WHAT EVERY
NEW
MANAGER
[NEEDS
TO KNOW]

WHAT EVERY
NEW
MANAGER
[NEEDS
TO KNOW]

MAKING A SUCCESSFUL
TRANSITION TO MANAGEMENT

GERARD H. (GUS) GAYNOR

AMACOM

American Management Association

New York • Atlanta • Brussels • Chicago • Mexico City • San Francisco
Shanghai • Tokyo • Toronto • Washington, D.C.

This publication is designed to provide accurate and authoritative information in regard to the subject matter covered. It is sold with the understanding that the publisher is not engaged in rendering legal, accounting, or other professional service. If legal advice or other expert assistance is required, the services of a competent professional person should be sought.

Library of Congress Cataloging-in-Publication Data

Gaynor, Gerard H.
    What every new manager needs to know : making a successful transition to management / Gerard H. Gaynor.
        p.   cm.
    Includes index.
    ISBN 0-8144-7179-X
    1. Management.   2. Leadership.   I. Title.

HD31.G3832   2004
658.4–dc21

2003010437

Printing number

10   9   8   7   6   5   4   3   2   1

To Shirley

Contents

[Preface]

WHAT EVERY NEW MANAGER NEEDS TO KNOW grew out of a concern that organizations continue to struggle in developing managers who are expected to take on demanding management responsibilities. During my tenure as a 3M executive I often faced the situation when a management position became available that someone would ask me: "I'd like to have my name put on the list." I usually responded with a rather simple question: "What have you done to prepare yourself for a position in management?" The response and subsequent discussion forced me to question just why and how this individual reached the conclusion to forsake a career as a competent discipline specialist and become involved in management.

From my experiences as an adjunct professor in management at the graduate level I find it troubling that few students fully understand what management involves. I also find that many students who have aspirations to pursue the management ladder have little if any knowledge of the demands placed on managers and of the scope of their responsibilities. They focus more on the tools of management than on the thought processes required to manage for both the short and long term. They also have relatively low levels of confidence in their immediate managers and don't see their managers as models to emulate or as proactive take-charge leaders.

When organizations need to fill such critical positions as managing the activities of others, why would they appoint people who are not adequately prepared? It is generally accepted that it takes years of schooling and practice to develop professionals in disciplines like science, engineering, finance, and law, but when it comes to the discipline of management people assume that anyone can manage anything without any formal preparation. Not so. The discipline of management is probably the most difficult of all disciplines: it involves dealing with human behavior, which doesn't follow some mathematical formula. This lack of preparation for a career in management may be the reason why the malpractice of management is so prevalent. Good management practice would suggest that some preparation in the discipline of managing would be an essential prerequisite. Yet to manage effectively and efficiently requires more than discipline knowledge: It requires understanding of management basics and human behavior supplemented with complementary attitudes, certain personal characteristics, and relevant experience.

The day-to-day leadership of an organization takes place in the trenches of the organization, where *managing activities* and dealing with the social interaction of all participants determine the future of the organization. This does not in any way demean the contributions of executive level management, but organizations meet their objectives through the efforts of the managers who deal directly with other internal organizational units, customers, suppliers, and government regulators. It is those mid-level managers who control the quality of the work effort: They determine whether the income and expense forecasts are met, they fulfill the organizational vision and objectives, and thus they are the key factor in success or failure. Yet organizations continue to appoint managers without fully evaluating their competencies or providing the necessary minimum education and training.

What Every New Manager Needs to Know focuses on the preparation that should precede appointment to a management position and on the learning that should take place in the first few years—the learning that comes not only from formal and informal education and training but also from the opportunities presented to gain experience. The book responds to some very basic questions involved in making a transition to management from a systems perspective:

❏ What does managing involve?
❏ What are the prerequisites for becoming a manager?
❏ How does one learn to be a manager?
❏ What are the challenges on the learning curve?
❏ What knowledge, competencies, skills, and attitudes are required?

❑ What are the major obstacles?

❑ What should be included in your managing model?

❑ What are the measures of a manager's performance?

What Every New Manager Needs to Know focuses attention on people who have a desire to become managers, whether they work in academia, government, industry, or not-for-profit organizations. The information in this book applies to the newly appointed managers who have little if any knowledge of what it means "to manage." It also applies to managers who have concluded that improving their managing competence is vital not only to their own future but to the future of the people whose activities they manage. Managers who need to improve their managing competencies may use this book to reappraise their current practices. Senior managers may be prompted to recognize that they have a responsibility for developing future generations of competent managers capable of dealing with opportunities and challenges yet to be discovered. And executives may begin to understand why the malpractice of management is so prevalent. *Management is about people.* Discipline competence by itself is insufficient to achieve expectations; results are obtained through the interaction of people.

What Every New Manager Needs to Know provides the tools and techniques needed to ease the transition to managing and the subsequent steps up the career ladder in management. Yet while the tools and techniques are important they take second place to learning the fundamentals of managing.

Chapter 1 raises the issues related to embarking on a career that determines the future of society and draws your attention to the need for integrating organizational purposes with people and processes.

Chapter 2 explores the seven management hats that every manager wears and which may require changing at a moment's notice.

Chapters 3 and 4 focus your attention on the critical people issues. Chapter 3 deals with staffing, career building, and enhancing career opportunities, and Chapter 4 covers managing individual and team performance.

Chapter 5 brings the people issues raised in Chapters 3 and 4 to the world of project management, with a focus on the up-front work.

If you are overworked, Chapter 6 helps you find the time to do your work and get the monkey off your back.

Chapter 7 considers leadership and communication from the entry-level perspective—*taking the lead* leadership—in meeting objectives and providing for future opportunities.

Chapter 8 provides insights into what it takes to think out of the box and then somehow transform that thinking into results.

Now that you've become a manager one of your responsibilities involves measuring performance. Chapter 9 provides some guidelines as to what needs to be measured and presents approaches for measuring not only your performance but also that of your organizational unit.

What is more important to you than managing your career? Chapter 10 should help you evaluate your knowledge, skills, attitudes, personal characteristics, and experience to become an effective manager of people's activities.

These ten chapters raise issues that you need to think about and think about deeply in the context of your personal ambitions. It's your career, and although managing has its enticements it must be approached with realistic expectations. Success in any discipline requires certain interests, talents, skills, and competencies. None of us possess them all. So we make choices, and I hope that *What Every New Manager Needs to Know* will help you make the choice to pursue the discipline of *managing* and be the best.

Acknowledgments

IT IS IMPOSSIBLE TO ACKNOWLEDGE all those individuals and in-teractions that over many decades have affected my career either directly or indirectly. My thinking and attitudes toward managing were fashioned by many people from across the globe—people who either through their action or inaction somehow made an impression and taught me a lesson-people from all skill levels and disciplines. Those casual conversations provided a source for learning and expanded my thought processes beyond the traditional and the casual.

The influences of family, friends, acquaintances, authors of books and professional journals, and of all those with whom I came in contact over these many years in one way or another influenced my thinking. Those teachings focused on a disciplined yet sensitive approach to people per-formance, effectiveness, and efficiency, on the need to do what I said that I would do, on not only resolving assigned problems but uncovering problems and new opportunities, and on taking responsibility for my own actions. I have been exceedingly fortunate in all my work experiences of having come in contact with people who pushed for excellence. Those learning experiences led me to a general operational philosophy of "there must be a better way" and that maintaining the status quo was generally not acceptable.

There is no way to mention or personally thank those many colleagues with whom I worked at all levels at 3M from around the globe that played a role in my career. My Italian and American colleagues in 3M Italy, where I worked for seven years, are entitled to a special note of thanks: My respect and friendship for them—world-class professionals.

My sincere thanks to AMACOM's editorial director, Ms. Adrienne Hickey, for her interest in promoting *What Every New Manager Needs to*

Know; to Mike Sivilli, the associate editor; and to Lydia Lewis, the production manager. It was my privilege and pleasure to work with a staff that demonstrated their professionalism in making *What Every New Manager Needs to Know* a reality.

Finally, to my wife Shirley, my partner who joined me in the decision to write this book, my sincere thanks for her interest and counsel, which were so essential for this effort.

WHAT EVERY
NEW
MANAGER
[### NEEDS
TO KNOW]

CHAPTER 1

Getting Started as a Manager

You are about to embark on a career that determines the future of society. Every failure and every success in academia, government, or industry can be traced to a manager's performance. The management creed places final responsibility and accountability for results on the manager. Henry Mintzberg[1] reminds us that:

> No job is more vital to our society than that of the manager. It is the manager who determines whether our social institutions serve us well or whether they squander our talents and resources.

Although Mintzberg made that statement in relation to upper management it applies equally if not more importantly at the entry and developmental management levels. Is Mintzberg placing too much emphasis on the role of the manager in society? Certainly not, if we accept the premise that managers are responsible for achieving results. A cursory review of the daily media gives many examples of managers who failed in their responsibilities with significant negative consequences to the organization's stakeholders and to society. An organization's success depends on how its resources, infrastructure, and culture are managed: its identity and its standing in the world community are built from the bottom up. The integration of activities throughout the organization and within each of the organizational subunits determines the organization's future. How we fulfill Mintzberg's challenge depends on how we perceive the function of managing.

MAKING THE DECISION

So you're about to embark on a career in management. In the past you considered the possibility of seeking a position in management but did not actively pursue it. You had a good standing as a professional contributor among your peers and managers and really didn't focus too much on management. Then a few weeks ago you had a discussion with an upper-level manager about the possibility of being appointed manager of your current department.

You discussed the responsibilities and some of the difficulties in making the transition. The discussion was introspective and provided you with an opportunity to gain some insight into the demands of the position. You recognize that the only management experience you have comes from serving as a project manager. That is quite different from taking total responsibility for the activities of the fifteen people who will be reporting to you directly and interacting with other professionals and managers from supporting disciplines if you become the department manager. You also know that others are being considered for the position.

As you thought about the idea you concluded that you probably possess the talent and some of the attributes associated with becoming a manager. You reflected on managers with whom you worked over the years as a professional and thought about what kind of manager you might be.

You've worked with good and not-so-good managers but with only one that you really thought met your standards as a model manager.

Deciding to become a manager is not an easy decision for you because you are aware of the commitment of time and energy the position requires. This is not an eight-to-five job, but as a professional you have worked longer than eight to five on many occasions. You considered the various scenarios that might affect your lifestyle and your family and personal relationships if chosen for the position—traveling more, dealing with people's idiosyncrasies, bringing work home to meet deadlines, leading your professional peers, taking responsibility for group results, learning to work with upper management, serving on organizational committees, possibly transferring to another city in the future and maybe even accepting an overseas assignment, and learning what it means to manage. All of these factors determine your chances for success. You also thought about how you might make a greater contribution to the organization by taking a leadership role in determining its future directions—a possibility that could be exciting and provide an opportunity to have more voice in the organization. You gave all these issues serious thought, and decided to inform the manager of your definite interest in the position. More interviews and discussions followed.

More than a week has gone by since the final interview, and your mind has wandered at odd moments with thoughts about your possible appointment and its implications for your career. Now it's Friday morning and you arrive early as usual. Before noon the manager making the appointment informs you that you have been selected to replace the current manager as of Monday morning. He plans to get the group together around 4:00 P.M. for the announcement but requests that you don't publicize it, not even to your spouse. You haven't asked and you haven't been told why your current manager is being replaced. You don't know whether he is being replaced for poor performance or is receiving a new appointment. But you have a fair idea that his performance might be considered less than acceptable. You're on cloud nine, and you once again go over all the reasons that you accepted the position, but wonder whether you made the right decision.

When 4:00 P.M. arrives, the group meets in the conference room. After a few comments by the appointing manager and a bit of levity, he announces the reason for the meeting. Of course, almost everyone knew for a couple of weeks that something was going to happen because they saw office doors being closed when most of the time they're left open. The manager talks about the goals of the organization and past performance and finally announces that you've been appointed the new department manager as of Monday morning. There's a nonverbal mixed reaction and the manager asks everyone to cooperate with you during this transition and concludes with a few general remarks. As the meeting breaks up most of the group offer their congratulations. So here you are; it's Friday at 5:00 P.M. and on Monday at 8:00 A.M. you will put on a management hat for the first time. Where do you start?

You have now been appointed to the NEW MANAGER'S CLUB, which includes all those competent professionals who enter the management ranks without any formal education or training as to what managing includes.

WHY WAS THE POSITION OPEN?

You accepted the position, but did you ask why this appointment was necessary? Why the position became available is one of the most important questions to be asked, especially if you're replacing a manager who has not met expectations. The manager who appointed you will not be willing to go into extensive detail. So learn what you can but don't press the issue too far.

Vacancies generally arise from one of three circumstances: the current manager is promoted, the current manager does not meet the requirements, or a new group is being organized. Major organizational restructurings do occur but are beyond the scope of these guidelines for the new manager. You will face only moderate difficulties in making the transition from specialist to manager if the current manager either receives a promotion or is transferred to a comparable position to gain new experience. Under these circumstances you can probably assume that the group was generally well managed and no major undiscovered issues will arise—with an emphasis on *major undiscovered issues*. Although there will be less effort required to learn the inner workings of the group, you'll face the problems generally associated with making a transition. Eventually you'll put your own signature on the group's direction and focus.

If the current manager is being replaced because of poor performance, your transition could be more difficult. How you respond depends on the particular set of problems. Do they relate to morale, lack of professional competence, the wrong mix of skills, or just prior ineffective management? You'll also need to have an understanding of the expectations of the group you have inherited. Does your manager now have the courage to create change or does he or she prefer to work around the periphery, talking about needed change but not really supporting it. Changing how the group you inherited operates may be difficult if your manager chooses to be overly cautious and becomes concerned about upsetting too many people. You need to learn very quickly that people will resist even minor changes but implementing the necessary changes is part of your leadership function. You'll need to find a way to implement the changes that you and your organization consider essential.

If you're appointed as manager of a new group you'll have an opportunity to grow into the position more easily. You may have an opportunity to select some of your staff, establish the direction, and define the scope of the work. A new group with a specific purpose and objectives does not usually begin with a large staff. You'll find that new groups emerge and grow after small results begin showing promise. Your challenges lie ahead of you and how you respond will determine your success. You can expect some verbal flack because you'll probably be encroaching on other protected territory. Once positive results become apparent the opposition will jump on the bandwagon and make claim of their support from day one. Don't waste any time protesting; it's part of the price you pay for pursuing a leading-edge effort. Unfortunately too many young managers refuse such appointments because of the unknowns. In most cases they would be charting new directions and plowing new ground. It takes a person who is comfortable with taking risks and living with uncertainties to give birth to a new idea.

As a newly appointed manager you also need to have an understanding with your manager about the following issues:

1. Purpose of the group
2. Expectations for the group
3. Competencies within the group

4. Interaction with other organizational subunits

5. Specific areas of responsibility and accountability

6. Subunit's annual budget

7. Manager's general philosophy of operation

8. Communication protocols with your manager and other subunits

9. Education and training programs available

10. Your limits of authority

Some of these answers will be available as a result of discussions with your manager but others may surface on that Monday morning when you begin a career as manager.

GETTING STARTED

Now that you've joined the ranks of those who manage let's consider the issues that will help you develop some managing principles and a system of thought—a philosophy of managing. Without a guiding philosophy, your thinking will have to begin at the bottom of the learning curve for every issue that arises. You can't simply afford to restart the engine every time a major issue arises. You need to develop some operational philosophy that will guide you through the maze of decision-making processes. The real world of the entry-level manager is quite different from that presented in the academic or business press. The quick fixes presented by the management gurus to executive-level managers do not lead to management utopia. You're dealing with people who bring all their uniqueness to the workplace, and their skills and abilities must somehow be integrated to meet the organization's purposes.

You are now part of the organization's management team regardless of your past professional discipline or your organizational function. Your domain of operations has changed, and you now must view the organization from a broader perspective. You are on the other side of the desk, with responsibility for the performance of others. Throughout this book the word *organization* will include those in academia, government, industry, and the not-for-profit world. It will apply to every discipline on the continuum from the humanities to science and engineering, to every type of organization whether national or global, to every organization whether product or service oriented, and to every organization from the smallest to the largest.

MANAGEMENT AND MANAGING: IS THERE A DIFFERENCE?

Management as a practice is part of ancient history, but management as a discipline is a mid-twentieth century invention. A review of the literature will find many descriptions for the activity we call management. The word *management* used as an impersonal inclusion of some unidentified body of decision makers has no meaning. Managers are part of management and thus responsible for results through *managing*. Management also includes a body of knowledge and is a discipline that has theories, although they are not governed by the laws of science.

Research results from the academic community provide the manager with new insights to be used in the process of managing. While those insights may not be fully quantified they need to be explored for the hidden gems. Peter Drucker in *The Essential Drucker*[2] asks the question: "Is management a bag of *techniques and tricks*?" It appears so after scanning the books and periodicals from the academic and business press that focus on techniques and tools for managing. But management is more than tools and techniques—it's a body of knowledge that supports the act of managing.

Managing could be described as applying the theories of management. But that description lacks specificity; theories are applied to what, and for what purpose? Managing has also been described as *being responsible for the work of others*. True, but not sufficiently inclusive. Managing is about *people*—how to develop skills and competencies that meet the needs of the organization and provide opportunities for personal growth. For our purposes, consider managing as *the practice, the art, and the act of doing*. Responsible managers meet the organization's objectives and fulfill their commitment to the organization *by managing*. To restate Drucker's description: Managing is not a bag of tools, techniques, and tricks; it is about human beings. Its task is to make people capable of joint performance, to make their strengths effective and their weaknesses irrelevant.

My emphasis throughout this book will focus on expanding the position from which the manager views the function of managing. Managing involves more than meeting the objectives for your group; managing also involves guaranteeing that meeting your objectives is in consort with the objectives of other groups. This applies to those involved in academia, government, or industry. You need to be able to communicate effectively and understand each other. As a manager your scope of operations expands and your actions and decisions impact other groups. If you're a manager in marketing or sales, you need to understand some level of the technology involved in order to communicate effectively with customers. If you're a manager in the finance department, you're not simply a book-keeper; you should provide insight, establish guidelines, and look for ways to find the workable financial solutions. You are managing part of the organizational resources and those resources include not just people and money but also the intellectual property, technology, time, distribution channels, customers, suppliers, production capability, operating facilities, finance, and all external resources.

MANAGING PEOPLE OR MANAGING ACTIVITIES

From my personal experience and observations I suggest that you cannot manage people—you manage their activities and through that process help them become effective contributors to meeting the organization's objectives. Managing people implies some level of command and control—do what I tell you to do, the way I want it done, and within the time that I think it should be done. Of course there are many levels of command and control, but its use should be limited to crises that require making a decision without the opportunity for seeking input from others. In contrast, managing activities means that managers look at results and how they were achieved. They balance freedom and control to the extent required. They provide opportunities for independent action within appropriate limits.

What do we mean by managing activities? Every organization fulfills its mission by accomplishing well-defined goals directed toward meeting specific objectives. Those objectives are eventually broken down into various activities and assigned to individuals who possess the necessary competence to complete them. The completion of those activities involves expectations that are usually defined as outcomes or results. The focus must be on results achieved from engaging in specific activities that further the purposes of the organization. We also want to provide our employees an opportunity to contribute their knowledge, their creativity, and their skills toward completing those activities. That's why we brought them into the organization.

As an example, Mike has been given responsibility for developing one part of a business plan for a new program. Mike has all the required qualifications. The goals are clearly defined and a completion timeline has been established. Does Mike's manager tell him how to do his job? Definitely not. Does she review the job objectives so Mike understands both the requirements and any special conditions? Definitely yes. Does she only check his progress at appropriate intervals?

If Mike needs to be told how to do his job then evidently he doesn't possess the necessary education, experience, or skills. However, Mike doesn't need to possess all of the qualifications. Keep in mind that seldom will a person or group possess all the education, knowledge, and skills to perform some activity. There are usually gaps that must be accommodated. If Mike is moderately proficient, he has an opportunity for gaining experience if his manager takes the opportunity to teach, coach, and provide direction toward successful completion of the activity. There is no need for Mike to reinvent the wheel, so input from his manager should be expected and welcomed. Both Mike and his manager agreeing on the objectives and other requirements is absolutely essential; both must be playing off the same sheet of music.

Mike's manager must also check his progress: this may be formal or informal. It depends on the confidence and level of trust between Mike and his manager. How Mike's manager responds to his work depends on what factors determine the success of this specific activity, knowledge of how Mike's work integrates with other activities, and some understanding of the principles being applied by Mike. So, if Mike is moderately competent, has a desire to learn, demonstrates enthusiasm for the challenge, and fully understands the requirements associated with the activity, his manager has an opportunity to provide a career growth opportunity. But, she needs to work with Mike, and perhaps in the future it may be appropriate for her to check on his progress only periodically.

By focusing on managing activities rather than managing people we direct attention to what it takes to achieve a particular objective. We accept people as they are with all of their idiosyncrasies and focus on developing their talents by providing direction and allowing them to expand their competencies.

MANAGING WITHIN A CULTURE

No research is required to demonstrate that people are an organization's greatest asset and that organizational culture determines performance. Success in any organization comes from assembling a critical mass of people in the required disciplines and creating a culture that supports the group of unique individuals with all their foibles and idiosyncrasies.

So what is organizational culture? In my previous book,[3] I described organizational culture as: "including the shared values, the beliefs, the legends, the rituals, the past history, the intellectual and operational traditions, the pride in past accomplishments, the policies and practices, the rules of conduct, the organization's general philosophy of operation, and other artifacts that define the organization." There are two parts to this description: the behavioral and the emotional.

The behavioral aspects of an organizational culture include shared values, beliefs, intellectual traditions, policies and practices, rules of conduct, and philosophy of operation. The emotional aspects include the legends, rituals, past history, and pride in past accomplishments. While the behavioral elements may be granted greater significance because they are measurable, the emotional elements add the ingredients that generate the spirit and passion of the organization.

Organizational cultures span a continuum from the overcontrolled to the overpermissive. Overcontrolled cultures limit creativity and innovation, and overpermissive cultures seldom provide a sustaining organization. As practitioners in managing we know that most people need some level of control and relatively few can function effectively with total freedom. The manager's job is to balance control and freedom to the group and also to the individuals within the group.

Most discussions about culture focus on the macro-organization's culture, but the most important culture is the culture that you as a manager develop for your specific group. The organization will most likely promote a stated culture but the culture you develop for your group will depend on your needs, the activities and expectations assigned to your group, and the competencies and attitudes of the people. While senior management may promote creativity and innovation we would question just how much and how often we'd want creativity and innovation in the finance department. We'd question just how many productive mavericks should be in the payroll department. We have seen in recent years the disasters created by creative accounting. However, if you're managing a research, development, or marketing function, creativity and innovation may be the number one priority. This does not suggest that any organizational function can eliminate creativity and innovation from its vocabulary, but each function will need creativity and innovation of a different type, on a different scale, and guided by different principles. So although the organization may have principles that define its culture, you will develop a culture based on your people and your vision and direction as a manager.

MANAGING DIFFERENT NEEDS

While we like to talk about the uniqueness of the people that we associate with, we seldom consider their uniqueness in our working relations. Why is it that when we search for the best and the brightest and bring them into the organization that very often they do not meet our expectations? As an example, many organizations focus on hiring the top ten percent of the graduating class. Is that really necessary? If we assume that the top ten percent provide the best without any data to support such a decision we create problems for both the organization and the new hire. Academic credentials need to be supplemented with some minimum level of people skills—especially communication and leadership skills.

As a manager you need to know the competencies of your people and at what level they can participate most effectively. There are many different types of people in every discipline and every discipline covers a spectrum of individuals with specific knowledge, skills, attitudes, personal characteristics, and work and other experiences. Here are several continuums to reflect on when considering the placement of people:

- ❑ From the person who prefers routine to the change maker
- ❑ From the one satisfied with the status quo to the one who says *if it ain't broke, fix it*
- ❑ From the one who sees the trees to the one who sees the forest to the one who sees both the trees and the forest
- ❑ From the one who lives in the cubicle to the one who seeks broader experiences
- ❑ From the plodder to the proactive to the creative to the innovator
- ❑ From the one who thinks within the box to the one who thinks out of the box
- ❑ From the one who asks why to one who asks why not
- ❑ From the academically oriented to the practitioner to the one who functions in both the academic and practitioner camps
- ❑ From the thinker to the doer to the thinker and doer

You should recognize that a person who is hired to do research in any discipline and is then assigned to a routine activity will either fail or leave the organization. If you do this, you may participate in destroying a career. As an example, if you assign a change maker to the position that involves maintaining the status quo and vice versa you create a situation that will not only require hours of your time in the future but will also have a negative impact on performance. You create dissatisfaction that leads to lack of motivation. Careers can be destroyed through improper placement and such actions have a negative impact on performance. Managers need to reflect on these continuums to make appropriate assignments.

CAREER STAGES OF THE SPECIALIST

An undergraduate degree or some specialized vocational training does not endow professional status; it provides some basic knowledge and the keys to start the journey. After completing an academic program, we may be learned in our specialty and we may have even acquired an understanding of complex theories, but we only have untested knowledge. In most cases we have not used the learning in solving real problems that require interaction with not only other professionals but also many people both within and outside the organization. To achieve professional status we go through three basic stages. If you haven't moved into a responsible management position after fifteen years in your specialty, chances are you will remain a specialist. I have intentionally avoided linking stages to the traditional way of years of experience because we all bring different experiences to the workplace.

Stage 1

We begin our careers as apprentices even if we have an advanced degree, whether our profession involves research, development, finance, marketing and its related functions, or many other functions and disciplines. As professionals we don't like to be referred to as apprentices but that's what we are. The term applies to all fields of endeavor whether our organizations involve banking, healthcare, fast food, the arts, or any other professional fields. We're generally given direction, we're in a learning stage, and we may or may not contribute anything of significance to the total organizational effort. We'll probably also be asked to perform some mundane tasks. In these early days we'll often question the relevance of our assignments. Stage 1 provides us the opportunities to gain the necessary skills required to build a successful career; it's an opportunity to begin applying what we've learned.

Stage 2

This is the time to become an independent as well as a major team contributor to the total organizational effort. This is the time that we make the decision to be proactive and to be the pathfinders in directing the future or the benchwarmers waiting for the next assignment. This is where experience fortified by additional knowledge allows us to begin to make major contributions. We've paid some of our dues by performing many of those tasks that we thought were well below our educational level but later found the experiences useful. Stage 2 focuses on continued growth in our field of specialization and should include ever-increasing responsibilities. We now justify our existence by being able to take on total responsibility for some part of a well-defined project. We should no longer be told what to do; we should be making the proposals for what needs to be done to fulfill the organization's purposes and objectives.

Stage 3

In Stage 3 we begin to play the role of coach, mentor, and teacher to those entering Stage 1. We are now also expected to demonstrate initiative at the departmental level, use our creativity to improve operational processes, and be fully cognizant of the impact our activities have on other organizational units. We no longer depend on direction from others. We now are not only problem solvers but also can become problem finders. We are in a position to influence and to shape the organizational unit's direction, integrate our activities with those of other organizational units, and focus our activities for the benefit of the whole organization. Our scope of concern now becomes much broader. Lifelong learning in our own discipline and related disciplines will continue.

The lines between these three stages are fuzzy. How long one might remain in Stage 1 and function as an apprentice depends on what that person brings to the assignment. If book learning is your only achievement, then apprenticeship may take several years. If your vocation and avocation were essentially the same it's conceivable that you might even skip the apprenticeship stage on your first assignment. If you knew from early childhood just what you wanted to be chances are you gained the equivalent of that apprenticeship experience by participating in related activities.

So when do most people make that transition to management? It depends on many factors. I have witnessed Stage 1 people from various disciplines performing according to Stage 3 requirements—the accountants who function more like financial controllers than as bookkeepers, the marketers who recognize the complete product development system, the engineers and scientists who focus on the end use of a product rather than the elegance of the technology, and the people who approach their workload from an organizational perspective rather than a narrow functional or discipline perspective. Their prior experiences coupled with their personal characteristics gave them a head start. They are willing to go the extra mile and take some calculated risks and make some mistakes. Making mistakes is part of the learning process in any discipline. Their actions may come from perhaps not knowing better or from just sticking their necks out and disregarding the potential roadblocks to meet their commitments regardless of the amount of personal effort and inconvenience. These are the people who do not know that some particular task may not be able to be accomplished. These are the people that drive the future of the organization in their particular discipline or organizational function.

Success in any endeavor depends not only on education and experience that translates into knowledge but on the personal attitudes and traits that we bring to the table. We need to ask ourselves whether we seek a professional career or a job. A professional career demands high levels of personal commitment. While you may be new to the issues facing managers, your professional life really provided you with many opportunities to witness how other managers function. You at least learned what not to do as a manager.

FROM WHERE TO WHERE

Not all transitions to management present the same opportunities or problems; the effort required depends from where and to where the transition is being made. Generally the transition takes place in Stage 2 of the professional career. So let's explore the new requirements and possible points of entry into managing. Figure 1-1 shows some typical points of entry into *managing*. The basic organizational structure is broken down into the organization, divisions, a number of subunits that include various functions or disciplines, and projects. Points of entry include:

- ❑ Project manager (1) in your current subunit
- ❑ Manager of the subunit (2) in which you are currently assigned
- ❑ Project manager in a different subunit (3) in the same division

Figure 1-1. Basic organization chart.

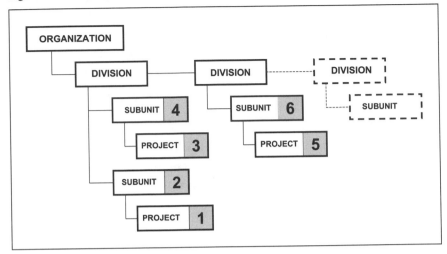

- ❏ Manager of a different subunit (4) in your current division
- ❏ Project manager in a subunit of a different division (5) in the same organization
- ❏ Manager of a subunit (6) in a different division in the same organization
- ❏ Project manager in a new organization (not shown)
- ❏ Manager of a subunit in a new organization (not shown)

Each of these points of entry presents challenges that require not only acquisition of new knowledge but also an understanding of human relations from the management perspective. You are no longer just one member of the group interacting with your peers. You now have responsibility for managing the activities of your peers and/or other professionals. So, let's explore these new requirements that depend on where you enter the management of the organization.

1. *Project Manager in Your Current Subunit*. This is probably the easiest transition since you will need little new knowledge about the function or discipline. The transition depends primarily on the personal relations you have with your project-

peers. You are no longer responsible solely for your contribution. Those duties related to administration, direction, and leadership now become important. Your responsibility now involves delivering a successful project. The main question: What do you know about managing?

2. *Manager of the Subunit in Which You Are Currently Assigned.* Here the transition becomes more complex. The new group may include from two to ten or more people and several projects that now involve working with managers from other functions and disciplines. New requirements are also added: human resource issues related to evaluating, hiring, coaching, reassigning, terminating, and educating; being the final arbiter in making decisions; developing financial forecasts; fulfilling department commitments into which you had no input and with which you may not fully agree; and directing the future of the subunit. An overriding issue that requires thought as well as diplomacy involves resolving the personal relations with your peers. You are no longer one of them; you are now responsible for their performance.

3. *Project Manager in a Different Subunit in the Same Division.* The comments in (1) apply here as well but moving to a different subunit adds new challenges. New operational knowledge will have to be acquired. The competence and idiosyncrasies of the staff are unknown. The question of why this stranger has been assigned will need to be resolved. Obviously the challenges will depend on the scope of the project.

4. *Manager of a Different Subunit in Your Current Division.* The issues raised in (2) apply and more. While your management potential has been recognized your knowledge of the function or discipline may be limited. Somehow you need to very quickly begin to understand the scope of operations, the problems associated with the group, and the competence of the assigned people. You may be going into new territory

where your reputation may not be known and the reasons why you were given this responsibility rather than a current member of the group will surface.

5. *Project Manager in a Subunit in a Different Division in the Same Organization*. The comments noted in (1) and (3) apply. As noted in (3) you may be going into new territory where your reputation may not be known, and these questions will be raised either directly or indirectly: Why was someone from outside the subunit selected? Why you? You'll need to demonstrate why you were appointed rather than someone from within the subunit. Your actions will determine your level of acceptance and you have about twenty-four hours to demonstrate your competence.

6. *Manager of a Subunit in a Different Division in the Same Organization*. The effort required to make a successful transition depends on why you were selected as the manager and why a new manager was required. Include all the issues raised from items (1) to (5) and more. There will be more to learn about operations and the challenge of working with a new group of people. We cannot minimize or disregard the human relations issues. There will be people in the group who will immediately begin to test your competence in dealing with the issues facing the subunit. You'll be given conflicting information about the nature of the problems. Some will try to curry favor. Others may take a wait-and-see attitude. Your success depends on your ability to read the environment.

7. *Project Manager in a New Organization*. Although not shown in Figure 1-1, it follows the same organizational pattern and includes all the comments from (1) to (6) and more. You are now in unknown territory. The people assigned to the project are unknown to you and you to them. The knowledge associated with managing the function or discipline may be new and getting on that learning curve quickly is important. You

need to keep in mind that you and the project manager are accountable for performance.

8. *Manager of a Subunit in a New Organization*. Although not shown in Figure 1-1, it follows the same organizational pattern and includes all the items from (1) to (6) and more. You're really on the bottom of the learning curve, dealing with new people, a new environment, new policies and procedures, and a new operational philosophy. Regardless of the interviews that led to the assignment you really don't know the organization. You don't even know the manager to whom you will be reporting; you know only how he or she conducts an interview. Those hidden factors quickly arise: How does your new manager communicate? What's his or her management style? What are the expectations? How much freedom do you have?

ORGANIZATIONAL STRUCTURE

All organizations provide either a product or service in some form that we'll refer to as a *result of some defined activity*. The words products and services usually become commingled because most products provide a service and most services also involve a product. A consultant's report involves a product and a service—a result. Insurance and financial institutions provide products and services—results. The arts and related activities such as symphonies, film, theater, literature, painting, and others provide a service through the use of products. Fast-food organizations provide a product and a service. The government provides products and services; building an infrastructure is both a product and a service—a result. Health-care services market their products to provide services.

All organizations operate within some form of structure. Figure 1-2 shows a generic functional structure for any organization and will be used as a model throughout our discussion on managing at the entry level. All the functions listed may not apply to any one organization, and they can be disregarded if not essential. All of these functions will have different levels of importance depending on the organization. The organizational model shown in Figure 1-2 includes three groups: genesis, distribution, and services.

Genesis

Genesis includes the basic functions of research, development, and production that play some role in every organization. The types of research will differ, and development may come from any discipline, but eventually something must be produced as a result of the research and development effort. That result may be a product, a service, a combination of a product and service, or some intangible benefit, but there will be a result from that activity.

Distribution

Distribution, which includes marketing, sales, physical distribution, and customer service, are common activities in all organizations. Distribution is more commonly associated with industrial organizations, but it applies to all organizations. The government, from the federal to the smallest entity, provides these functions, although not necessarily to our satisfaction. Academic institutions market, sell, and provide services to their customers, who are the students and the community. Arts-related organizations also market, sell, and provide a service to their customers and the community. All organizations, without exception, must provide some level of these four distribution functions.

Figure 1-2. Organizational functions.

Genesis	Distribution	Services
• Research • Development • Production	• Marketing • Sales • Physical Distribution • Customer Service	• Financial • Human Resources • Patent and Legal • Public Relations • Procurement • General Administration

Services

An organization's service functions provide all the ancillary work necessary to achieve some desired result. No organization can operate without them. Certainly financial and human resources are absolutely essential. Patent and legal services include trademarks, copyrights, and protection of intellectual property. Public relations, depending on the size of the organization, can be an organized function or handled by some designated person. And every organization requires assignment of the procurement function to some individual or group. The general administration classification includes all of those activities that we too often take for granted— benefits administration, internal and external communication services, custodial services, information and data processing, economic and other studies, fire and emergency evacuation, food services, library services, internal and external mail services, medical health and hygiene, transportation and travel services, and many others that we depend on for meeting our commitments as managers.

PURPOSES, PEOPLE, AND PROCESSES

The fundamentals of management follow a very simple model, as illustrated in Figure 1-3; *integrate purposes, people, and processes* (3Ps) with the available resources and supporting infrastructure. Management involves nothing more or less than managing activities directed toward some purpose and with the appropriate people and processes. Every organizational activity follows this pattern; a defined purpose implemented through people following certain predefined processes. This pattern fits all activities across a spectrum from making major organizational acquisitions at one end to the lowliest activity at the other end. If the purpose of the activity cannot be defined, then why pursue it? If the people with the right competencies are not available to pursue the activity, why dedicate the effort? Without the required people competencies processes provide no value.

This model applies to all organizational activities whether related to academia, government, industry, or not-for-profit organizations. It applies to all disciplines. It applies to all activities regardless of size, scope, or configuration. The 3P model that integrates well-defined purposes acted

Figure 1-3. Integrating purposes, people, and processes.

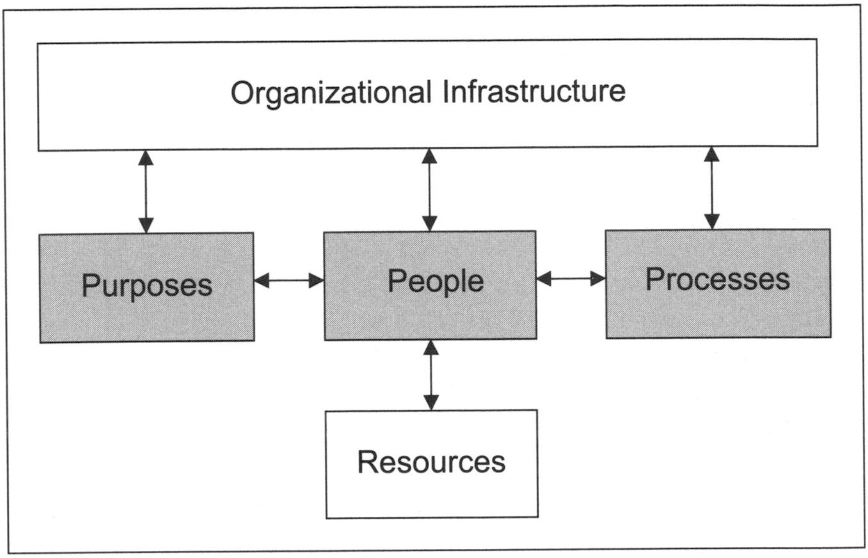

upon by competent people and adaptable processes provides the best opportunity for success in reaching objectives.

The 3Ps, while providing a simple management model, are difficult to implement. When we define purposes, select people, or develop processes we usually do not *develop right or wrong* answers; we develop the best approximations based on the available information that may be partially right and partially wrong or inconclusive. We judge information based on the credibility of the source. Doing an objective analysis without any bias is difficult to achieve. So success of the 3P model depends on the information used to define the purposes, people, and processes. It also depends on recognizing that the linkage of purposes, people, and processes is dynamic and that new information may require changes in the purposes, people, and processes.

TAKE A WIDE-ANGLE VIEW OF MANAGING

Your management style, focus, and motivation provide the driving force for your group. The purpose of an organization is not just to make money; the purpose is to provide positive results that generate a surplus and allow the organization to grow and meet its obligations to its various stakeholders. Making money is a result of investing resources in programs that add value to the organization. Over the years many books and articles have been presented to convince managers to focus on some single issue such as excellence, results, profit, performance, sustainability, or benefit to the community. We could add to this list other single issues such as strategic planning, reengineering, outsourcing, performance management, empowerment, and the other acronym-based panaceas that have come and gone without any long-term impact on the organization. Do these issues involve you as a newly appointed manager? Definitely yes.

You are now expected to contribute to the benefit of the whole organization. Just looking after your own subunit is insufficient. You now need to take a systems perspective and establish your subunit as a value-adding force to meet the goals and objectives not only of your subunit but also of the organization. You don't make progress in your career or in an organization by sitting on the sidelines. Something must happen to make progress. Focusing on any one single issue will not sustain an organization for the long term. All must be kept in balance, although one or more may have higher priorities depending on the circumstances. Consider each of the following single issues: excellence, results, profit, performance, sustainability, or benefit to the community.

1. *Excellence*. Excellence in which area of the organization? Excellence is a moving target. What was excellent yesterday may not even make the grade today. An organization cannot possibly be excellent in all operational areas unless the targets are lowered to such an extent that excellence has no meaning. So, decide how to pursue excellence and where it provides the greatest benefit.

2. *Results.* Results only become reality when the means for accomplishing them are included in the projections. Results require a defined system for measurement. The *how achieved* becomes important because short-term results can be achieved while destroying future capabilities and opportunities. Just what is meant by results needs to be defined and clearly communicated.

3. *Profit*. Profit, or surplus in the case of not-for-profit organizations, cannot be disregarded. A positive income stream compared to expenses is necessary to sustain the organization. But if profit becomes the only motivation then the organization may have other opportunities to provide the greatest return on investment. That could include entering new businesses, changing direction, or even closing operations.

4. *Performance.* Performance involves meeting the operational objectives of the organization. Those projects must meet three requirements: specifications, time schedule, and cost estimates. The supporting organizational functions must also meet their commitments.

5. *Sustainability.* Building the future of the organization provides many challenges because sustainability depends on the ability to satisfy many conflicting expectations: those related to internal and external entities. Long-term sustainability is often subject to forces beyond control of managers.

6. *Benefit to the Community*. Community responsibility is met when organizations provide jobs, meet the requirements of being good citizens, and contribute to volunteer-sponsored programs. However, in recent years we have seen the demise of organizations that have directed too many resources to meeting social needs of the community.

Successful managers balance these six factors. All are important. Without some effort in pursuing excellence organizations become mediocre. Without a positive surplus from operations the organization will soon be gone. Without a program in continuous improvement the organization will lose to its competitors. Without building for the future the organization puts itself, its employees, its customers, and its suppliers at risk. Without becoming a social presence in the community the organization creates untenable problems.

DEVELOPING YOUR APPROACH TO MANAGING

What kind of an organizational unit will you build—proactive, reactive, or inactive? There really is only one choice: proactive. Reactive units are always playing catch-up to the competition. Inactive units, meaning those that do not even react to the environment, should not be allowed to exist. Keep in mind that all organizations face internal and external competition. This applies to academia, government, industry, and not-for-profit organizations.

A proactive organization of any size and in any function pushes the envelope in every discipline to the extent required to develop its competitive advantage. Members of the group are not only cognizant of the leading edge activities in their discipline but know when and how to implement them. They use all of the available resources at their disposal to their advantage. They build the organization by developing high levels of individual competency that translate into organizational capability. By pushing the future they build a sense of professional excitement that becomes invigorating and contagious. Why an emphasis on building a proactive organizational unit? Can you really achieve any personal satisfaction from working in an organization that only reacts to its competitors? Losing the game is hardly a motivator.

It is possible to build a proactive attitude in an organizational unit that provides a continuous flow of creative ideas and in the process builds a sense of excitement. It's only necessary to develop an environment that allows for socialization and the free flow of information and ideas on improving work methods and performance. Our current levels of sophistication too often defer our attention from some very basic principles like simplifying work methods, using the appropriate tools, considering organizational and people relationships, and above all placing people in positions where their strengths provide the greatest benefit to the organization and at the same time provide opportunities for career growth.

The following guidelines help build a proactive organizational unit:

- ❏ *Set the goals*. As manager you and your staff set the goals but you take the lead. You define what you want the unit to be (some like to call this vision). You become the role model. People will take their behavioral cues from you.

- ❏ *Meet project requirements*. Meet the three project requirements: performance to specifications, on time, and at cost. Whether or not these requirements are met depends on you as the manager.

❏ *Propose new projects*. Only doing what is assigned is not a sufficient challenge for you and your staff. Most people have more to give than what's expected and it's this opportunity to propose new projects that keeps them and the organization vital.

❏ *Develop high standards of professionalism*. It's easy to become satisfied with past performance. Yesterday's performance may not be adequate today. You cannot allow your professionals to continue to survive with what they learned as students.

❏ *Take calculated risks*. How much risk will you take and how much will you allow your people to take? There are always risks associated with suggesting some new activity, with suggesting some new approach that goes against traditional thinking, with questioning senior authority. But remember the adage: no risk, no reward.

❏ *Foster innovation*. This may be your number one responsibility. Organizations cannot survive without innovation. Competition is real. Fostering innovation can only come from developing a culture that provides the freedom of action with operational discipline.

❏ *Develop a mental discipline*. Managing is about solving problems and searching for opportunities. The processes of thinking, clarifying issues, considering the pros and cons, sorting alternatives, and making decisions require a disciplined structure. Those decisions may be made on the elevator ride or during a casual encounter but need to be guided by a disciplined process.

❏ *Make timely decisions*. There is nothing more frustrating than waiting for a decision. How many times have you been asked as a professional to supply more information and then more information and more information? Don't inflict this frustration on those people that work with you.

❏ *Create dissonance*. Welcome the constructive mavericks. Neutralize or eliminate any destructive forces.

As a final reminder, don't fall into the trap of acting like the new kid on the block; you may be, but you're a manager now. Don't let anyone convince you to take it slow but also don't enter with the force of a bull in the china shop. If you were appointed on Friday afternoon you've had the whole weekend to put together a rough outline of how you're going to manage. What you bring to the table Monday morning will set the stage for the future. You are now responsible for the results of others. Do you provide the leadership or do you allow others to direct the future?

SUMMARY

❏ Mintzberg's challenge requires managers to understand that their actions determine how our social institutions use their assigned talents and resources.

❏ Making the decision to become a manager requires introspection and consideration of what is expected from managers.

❏ Candidates for management positions need to have a full understanding of what lies ahead if they accept a particular position.

❏ Developing personal management principles cannot be avoided. Decisions must be based on some principles and an identified system of thought. Every issue cannot begin at the bottom of the learning curve.

❏ There is a difference between management and managing. Managing involves *doing.*

❏ People cannot be managed but we can manage their activities. While the organization may boast of a particular culture, the culture you develop within your group will determine the value added by your group.

❏ People are unique and we must use those unique characteristics for the benefit of the unit and the person. Accepting the uniqueness of people involves working with them as individuals and not clones.

❏ Specialists pass through stages to become professionals. From which stage professionals join the ranks of managers depends on their personal characteristics and their ability to guide other people through successful careers.

❑ The ease with which a transition is made to manager depends on how far from the current organization the opportunity is offered.

❑ A simplified organizational structure applies to all organizations. There are only three components: genesis, distribution, and services.

❑ The fundamentals of managing involve the integration of purposes, people, and processes.

❑ Managing is not a single-issue exercise. There is no single panacea for success. Managing involves taking the systems approach.

❑ Taking a proactive approach and developing a proactive organizational unit that works on the leading edge of any discipline provides not only the best results but also the greatest satisfaction.

NOTES

1. Henry Mintzberg, "The Manager's Job: Folklore and Fact," *Harvard Business Review,* March–April 1990, Reprint 90210.
2. Peter F. Drucker, *The Essential Drucker* (New York: HarperCollins, 2001), pp. 10–13.
3. Gerard H. Gaynor, *Innovation by Design* (New York: AMACOM, 2002), p. 115.

CHAPTER 2

The Seven Management Hats

Making a transition to management requires understanding the basic functions of the manager. Figure 2-1 shows the manager's work from

Figure 2-1. The seven management hats.

ADMINISTRATION HAT—managing the nuts and bolts

DIRECTION HAT—teacher, coach, promoter, and innovator

LEADERSHIP HAT—taking the lead

PEOPLE HAT—understanding human behavior

ACTION HAT—the hands-on work

HIGH-ANXIETY HAT—the challenging work

BUSINESS HAT—where it all comes together

seven basic perspectives—the seven management hats. Three hats describe the indirect workload and include administration, direction, and leadership. Four other hats describe the direct workload and include the people hat, the action hat, the high-anxiety hat, and the business hat. On your first day as a manager, you'll have administrative work that must be completed, you will provide direction to some of your people, and you will probably be expected to take the lead on some issue. You will have interaction with different kinds of people behaviors, there will be some challenging work, you may need to resolve a serious conflict, and you may be involved in activities at the organizational level that require putting on the business hat. This situation will continue as long as you remain in a managing position. As you become involved in the managing process you will recognize that you may change these hats many times during a typical workday. So let's look at these seven hats that managers wear, the expectations that go with them, how the expectations change as the occasion demands, and how managers develop an appropriate balance.

THE ADMINISTRATION HAT: MANAGING THE NUTS AND BOLTS

Doing administrative work is generally not considered to be the most exciting role of a manager unless by chance you receive some great satisfaction from dealing with routine details. The claim that there's not much room for creativity depends on whether you accept the status quo or decide that there must be *a better way* to accomplish those routine tasks. The objective is to move the paperwork through the paper mill, which has become a combination of paper and some form of electronic communication. This is the grunt work: the work that most professionals and managers despise, but doing it is not a choice. The paperwork essential for running an effective organization must flow efficiently through the system: policies and procedures and certain requirements must be met. Reports must be written but you must ask if they really serve a purpose. Expense vouchers need to be approved. The paperwork involved in hiring, evaluating, promoting, reassigning, and possibly dismissing personnel must be processed. Meetings need agendas. All administrative processes must be updated. Interfacing with other functions becomes imperative. In addition, certain organizational mandates require compliance. If as an example the organization decides to install flexible scheduling, you probably will comply whether or not you favor the policy.

Managers do have an opportunity to be innovative and eliminate many of the administrative details that not only do not add value but also consume resources that could be used more effectively for other work. However, managers must avoid becoming totally consumed by these activities. They are important but there are people who can perform many of these functions with far greater efficiency than the manager and they should be given the opportunity to do so.

THE DIRECTION HAT: TEACHER, COACH, PROMOTER, INNOVATOR

In providing direction, managers integrate knowledge, skills, attitudes, personal characteristics, and experience of the unit into an effective and efficient team. Providing direction involves managing the assigned and available resources within the limits of the organizational infrastructure. The resources include people, intellectual property, information, organizational attributes, technology, time, customers, suppliers, plant and equipment, facilities, and financial. The organizational infrastructure includes purposes, objectives, strategies, organizational structure, guiding principles, policies and practices, management attitudes, management expertise, support for innovation, acceptance of risk, communication, and social responsibility.

Integrating the available resources within the organizational unit's culture includes many different managerial activities, as shown in Figure 2-2.

Figure 2-2. Issues in providing direction.

Focusing		
Communicating	Teaching	Pulling
Integrating	Training	Analyzing/Synthesizing
Monitoring	Coaching	Negotiating
Motivating	Pushing	Promoting

This list may lead you to believe that becoming a manager involves more than could be expected of any human being. But a close look at the list shows that in our personal lives we already demonstrate some of these competencies but under different circumstances. Focusing on the following activities in meeting objectives allows you to develop a competent staff that meets current as well as future requirements. In the process you provide opportunities for growth. Focus the group but provide the flexibility when required.

❑ *Communicating up, down, laterally, within, and outside the organization—verbal, written, graphic, reading, and listening is critical*. One size does not fit all. The message must meet the needs of the listener. See Chapter 7 for a full discussion of communication issues.

❑ *Integrating the multifunctional interests of the group is important*. The disciplinary silos need to be brought together. Integrate the activities of various participating disciplines in the very early stages of a project or program. Track requirements and the performance so as to avoid future costly rework.

❑ *Progress cannot be monitored from the office*. Instead of only a show-and-tell try a *show-and-tell-and-see-and-feel* approach. Whether the work requires creative thought that ends in a document or a design that involves a product, take the time to view the physical results. Adopt a show-me attitude.

❑ *Motivating individuals and groups is essential*. But be cautious about using the motivational gurus; their impact lasts about 48 hours. Find a way to unlock individual self-motivation. This can usually be accomplished by developing an environment that lives on self-motivation. Most people do an acceptable job when given an assignment, but the self-motivated find the assignment and pursue it with a passion.

❑ *Teaching is part of the manager's role*. Teaching is not micromanaging. Everyone doesn't have to start at the bottom of the learning curve. You have experience (intellectual property), and you should pass it on and then allow your people to make new mistakes and learn from them and communicate them to others.

❏ *Training determines the future of your unit.* Experience is a great teacher but a little education can save a lot of time, effort, cost, and frustration. The cut-and-dry method can work with simple one-dimensional problems but most problems are more complex and require multidisciplinary knowledge.

❏ *Coaching applies to both the discipline side and the performance side of the person.* Discipline competence (the hard skills) is insufficient: it must be augmented by what most consider soft skills; I prefer to refer to them as integrating skills. The skills that make the discipline competence possible are the ones that involve working with people.

❏ *Pushing some people to accomplish their goals is necessary.* People who require continual attention and stroking need to be weaned from such behavior because it is not only detrimental to the performance of the group but also to the person who becomes the focus of unnecessary attention.

❏ *Pulling is quite different from pushing.* Helping a person through the difficult stages of a project either by providing input directly or from other sources builds confidence and trust. The manager who puts the person on the right path gains respect and at the same time helps move the project toward completion.

❏ *Analyzing without synthesizing provides only half the answer and often leads to indecision rather than action.* Synthesis involves bringing information from all those analyses and integrating them to reach an acceptable decision. Too much analysis leads to paralysis.

❏ *Negotiating requires the ability to know when to change course.* Everything is supposedly negotiable, but how far? Win–win may be a good concept but the fundamentals of any discipline cannot be disregarded. Too much compromise can lead to future problems. It's better to start over and look for new solutions.

❑ *Promoting, while not in the vocabulary of most profession-als and young managers, becomes a vital skill*. New ideas, concepts, and proposals that deviate from traditional prac-tices require salesmanship. Acceptance of anything new gen-erates some conflict, as it should. The proponent makes the case and the decision makers react. Questions will be asked so you need to do your homework.

THE LEADERSHIP HAT: TAKING THE LEAD

Leadership is the third component of managing. There are those who make a distinction between managing and leading. While leadership is vital, it is only one part of the management process. Leadership doesn't work in isolation to meet organizational objectives. Keep in mind that we're considering leadership as it applies to the *in-development* manager. Rather than trying to define leadership, let's consider leadership as *taking the lead*. See Chapter 7 for a full discussion of leadership. Leadership involves pathfinding; it involves defining where the organization is going and what it wants to be; it involves looking into the future; it involves going beyond the traditional opinions and rituals and it is not jumping on the bandwagon of the latest management guru. So here is a list of attributes that apply not only to the entry-level manager but to all managers:

❑ *Accept responsibility and accountability*. The rose must be pinned on someone. There can be no scapegoats; you are the manager and you are accountable. You can't blame your people for nonperformance. It's not easy when some person fails to perform, but you were there; it was your responsibility.

❑ *Don't kill the messenger*. Bad news will arrive and you need to deal with it. Although bad news is difficult to accept, if it is accepted immediately it creates a minimum negative impact. Time really is of the essence.

❑ *Make judgments based on an acceptable level of facts*. Lead-ers can't wait until all the facts have been accumulated. Some minimum amount of information is required. The rest is judgment. All the available sophisticated models, simulations, and computer programs may or may not help in making the decision.

☐ *Make the complex simple*. Make the complex easy to understand. The essence needs to be communicated. This is easier said than done since simplifying requires a great deal of disciplined thinking. But any issue that cannot be drawn down to its simplest essentials probably isn't understood.

☐ *Follow through with clear decisions*. Eliminate any hidden meanings. The decision may not be acceptable, but it must be understood. Acceptance involves understanding the impact of the decision and the implications of the decision on operations.

☐ *Challenge the so-called experts*. Experts have their place, but they also have their agendas. They may be experts of the past and not focused on the future. Their past experience and knowledge may or may not be useful. Above all be cautious of the single-issue experts who promote their panaceas.

☐ *Develop a proactive philosophy*. Leaders exhibit a proactive stance. It's too late to become proactive when the emergency arises. That emergency may have been avoided if someone had listened or someone had opened their eyes to the world around them. Anticipate future problems. Don't wait to be told what to do.

☐ *Obsolete the present before its time*. It's difficult to obsolete products, processes, and activities that at one time provided significant benefit. It's more difficult to obsolete thinking that no longer adds value. It takes courage to eliminate those great contributions made by some person now in upper management. Timely obsolescence prevents future crises.

☐ *Promote a positive attitude*. Look for solutions, not scapegoats. Blame only creates discord and destroys relationships. It doesn't solve problems. Those responsible must be held accountable, but the problem requires a solution. Focus on resolving the problem.

THE PEOPLE HAT: UNDERSTANDING HUMAN BEHAVIOR

The people hat involves gaining an understanding of human behavior. The uniqueness of people needs to be taken into account in developing plans and in making decisions that involve people. Managers very quickly find themselves in a position to make decisions that have current as well as future consequences.

☐ *Selecting the appropriate staff takes time*. It cannot be done in a perfunctory manner. Business success depends on professional competence coupled with well-developed nontechnical skills. Workload requirements cannot be met without the competencies required by defined purposes and objectives of the organization.

☐ *Hiring the right people involves knowing the expectations*. The workload requirements, the expectations, the specific assignment, the complementary fit with the mix of people already in place, and potential assignments determine the type of person to be hired.

☐ *Appraising employees and colleagues realistically requires judgment*. Effective employee appraisal frustrates most managers. The options include the normal distribution curve, everyone's a star performer, team appraisal, or individual performance. Personnel appraisal is serious business. You're either building or destroying a career.

☐ *Developing people competencies involves recognizing individual training needs*. Generalized programs where one approach fits all seldom provide real learning experiences. People are unique and need to be treated differently but above all don't forget simple respect and courtesy. At the same time expectations must be continually raised and excellence in performance cannot be compromised. Adults are not children, so treat them as adults.

☐ *Investing in people involves more than sending them to formal educational programs and providing additional perks*.

The results of that education need to be applied. Investing your time to coach, educate, and provide direction may be far more important than formal programs.

❏ *Tolerating mistakes that provide new learning cannot be avoided.* It's not necessary to break out the champagne and celebrate mistakes but let's learn from those costly mistakes. Creativity and innovation are fraught with false starts and mistakes that support the learning process as we enter the unknown. If mistakes were the exception rather than the rule, much of our effort could be diverted to develop a society where effectiveness, efficiency, and the economic use of resources would dominate our lifestyle.

❏ *Listening is difficult.* It is especially difficult when so much of what we have to *say* is obviously of greater importance. Listening requires discipline. You cannot spend the day listening to people who have not given any thought to the message they wish to convey. Listening is a two-way street—listen, yes, but know when to ask that the thoughts be written and explored in depth before any further dialogue takes place.

❏ *Developing people skills crosses through all disciplines.* Excessive praise or criticism often creates conflict. Praise that is specific and used judiciously can be a force for spurring on the group. But, avoid the generalities. Saying "Great job!" to John or Mary is often a meaningless gesture. Timely and constructive criticism of actions provides learning opportunities but such criticism should be done in private and not become personal.

❏ *Welcoming new ideas or proposals determines the future of your unit.* Insist that ideas be presented in writing. Ideas are plentiful but only of value if explored. Untested ideas remain in the bank of untested ideas—they don't add value. Ideas presented in written form have a better chance for implementation. Writing forces thought, and thought clarifies and raises issues that need to be resolved.

❏ *Saying no to a request may be the best answer.* Can you decide which requests you'll answer? Unless you learn to decide which requests are valid and which can go unanswered you'll be inundated with requests that you're not able to comply with. There will not be enough time.

❑ *Attending the organizational rituals provides an opportunity to gain a further understanding of how people communicate away from the workplace*. Attending them is not a matter of choice. Your presence will be expected. You owe it to your people.

❑ *Understanding the culture allows you to accept it, move it in some new direction, and develop a totally new culture*. If you accept it, you share the good and the bad. If you move it in some higher level with minor changes you'll probably face minor problems. If you choose to develop a totally new culture be aware that you need a new strategy and time to implement it with some changes in personnel. Culture affects your style of managing. An innovator cannot function in a brain-dead organization. A plodder will not survive in an innovative organization, at least not for long.

The people part of managing is probably the most difficult in making the transition to management—everything appears in shades of gray. There are no stock answers for resolving people-related issues. Bridging your own philosophy with that of colleagues and the specific organization may at times prove to be difficult.

THE ACTION HAT: DOING THE WORK

The action hat describes some of the real work of the manager. As a professional you have probably heard a lot about managers delegating. While managers do delegate many activities, there are others that require a full understanding and cannot be delegated. For the inexperienced manager these activities may seem not only extremely challenging but a total departure from the experiences as a specialist. They involve:

❑ Reviewing and understanding the workload
❑ Reviewing the people competencies
❑ Linking competencies to workload
❑ Developing budgets and forecasts
❑ Focusing on the customer
❑ Managing the manager's work

Reviewing and Understanding the Workload

Reviewing the project workload involves gaining a basic understanding of the scope, the deliverables, and the current status; the status related to fulfilling the requirements such as meeting specifications, time schedules; and the estimated and projected cost. So how does a newly appointed manager review the workload to gain an understanding of all the projects and their importance? This is the nitty-gritty part of managing: digging through those printed or electronic files and learning the scope and priorities of the workload.

There are basically two options: review the projects by reading the original project proposals and the follow-up reports or asking the project principals for a live overview; no fancy presentations, just come in and talk about the projects. A combination of these two options seems to be the most effective; a cursory review of the available project information followed by a disciplined project review by those responsible for the project. While all projects need to be reviewed, some may have a greater urgency and receive top priority. The manager to whom you report will most likely provide some guidance.

How you decide which projects to review depends on the organization and the scope of the projects. Some may already have a red flag attached; someone in the organization may be screaming. The review could be prioritized in various ways such as the amount of funding, the number of people involved, the urgency, and the impact on results. Projects that impact performance should receive top priority. It is best to decide on a process rather than turning those files over and over. Set up a procedure and follow it.

Reviewing the People Competencies

Involving the project leader and others in the review process also provides an opportunity to begin learning about the people. This is the time to begin understanding the human side of your responsibilities. The interchange allows you to gain some insight into the unit's competencies. This insight will help you make judgments about the capabilities and limitations of the staff that will be vital to the unit's success.

The current trend suggests that judgments should be avoided but that too often leads to mismanagement. As a manager you will make judgments. Success depends on judgments about people and their interactions, strategy, vision, and all those activities in which you'll be involved. While you need to be cautious about placing too much emphasis on first impressions, realize that they do play a role in managing. You can't sit on the fence waiting to see which way the wind is blowing. Stick to the facts and keep your comments impersonal. You're judging performance of people, processes, and results. This is the beginning of building relationships. This first contact should provide you with some insight into the people. It's not just a matter of finding out about the project but also something about the people involved.

As you become involved in this managing function you'll begin to know the people and appraise their specific competencies. One of the easiest ways to start this process is to review the personnel appraisal forms from the past few years. You may find that these past appraisals reveal more about the person who wrote the appraisal than about the one being appraised. Keep that in mind as you go through the process. These appraisals provide background only and must be viewed with some degree of skepticism. If you develop a distribution curve of your staff based on the appraisals, you'll find that the majority will be rated very high. Review those comments on each individual to find the depth in those appraisals. Look for what was not included as well as what was included. A review of these appraisals establishes a benchmark as you begin to have personal discussions with each of your people.

Where do you begin to find out what your people are capable of doing, their limitations, and where they really shine? You won't accomplish this by only reading reports. You need face-to-face conversation. If your people have been out of school five or more years don't place too much emphasis on academic credentials. You need to find out what they've accomplished, not what the team or group accomplished, but what they personally contributed during their period of employment. These exploratory conversations whether formal or informal help you determine how employees see themselves and their role in the group; what opportunities should be provided for career growth and added breadth of experiences; and what interests and motivates the person. Does this person function better in short- or long-term projects? Is this person a self-starter? Does this person look for better ways to accomplish their work? Does this person meet commitments in spite of the difficulties that might have appeared? How does this person interact with peers and related managers? Does this person exhibit any managerial characteristics that should be developed? You can only make decisions regarding the proper placement and expectations from any person after you've gained some understanding of their knowledge base, skills, attitudes, personal characteristics, experiences, and interests.

I cannot overemphasize that you fully understand not just the competencies available but also the competencies required to fulfill the unit's objectives for the current and projected workload. Does the right mix exist? The response to these questions usually requires further investigation. You do not necessarily search for this information with specific plans but obtain it through observation, project reviews, and personal discussions while providing input to projects, and knowing what is going on in the organization.

Developing new competencies within an existing staff does not present problems as long as people are willing to meet new educational requirements. What do you do with those who refuse? The options are not particularly palatable either for you or the individual involved. The options include transfer to another department or even possible dismissal, but don't slough off the responsibility by faking the individual's performance record. A transfer may just prolong the agony for the individual and the organization. Dismissal may be difficult because prior managers really never faced up to the person's limitations and took the easy route and overrated performance. Resolving such an issue often creates a dilemma. You may ask yourself, how can I dismiss this person? The objective answer is simple: dismiss if necessary. Your responsibility is to give the person every possible opportunity to improve performance. You provide the person with alternatives. If the person refuses, you have no alternative but to dismiss. In reality you may be doing the person a favor. But the dismissal must be based on facts and not just personal preferences.

As a manager who faced such situations on several occasions, I found that the properly addressed dismissal based on lack of performance and refusal to take advantage of opportunities to improve performance forces people out of their lethargy and puts them on a new career path. After the initial shock to the ego the majority of these people realized their shortcomings and found new opportunities within the limitations of their competencies.

Linking Competencies to Workload

The complexity involved in gaining insight into the unit's workload and competencies will vary depending on the assignment. Chapter 1 identified some entry points for the new manager. Linking workload and competencies always presents a challenge to new managers. The juggling act begins now. You have defined the project workload and know the competencies required to fulfill that workload. But you quickly realize that in making assignments that you don't have the right mix. You need two more people like Mary and at least one more like John, but you really don't need Katy or Mike. So what is the answer? Rescheduling projects may or may not be a viable solution. Eliminating certain requirements might be considered but that requires time to gain approval. Seeking resources from either other internal or external groups does provide a possible solution. Evaluating work methods and assignments also provides additional opportunities.

There are no simple answers and all the options depend on the extent of the imbalance between competencies that are needed to competencies available. Can part of Mary and John's workload be broken down so others can help fill the gap? Mary and John will probably say no. But as a manager you need to analyze the problem and determine if this is an alternative and an opportunity for others to participate and gain new experiences. But what do you do about Katy and Mike? They're competent in their field but you don't need them. If Katy and Mike have track records of successful performance you probably will not find any difficulties in transferring them to other groups. If the organization no longer has use for their competencies the only alternative may be dismissal with appropriate considerations.

But there's another opportunity that is too often forgotten. The organization has a major investment in Katy and Mike. They are a known quantity. Can their competencies be utilized in other areas with some additional education and training? Have you looked at your future needs and will the competence be there when it's needed? It may be time to provide Katy and Mike with some new opportunities.

Developing Budgets and Forecasts

There are significant differences between budgets and forecasts. Budgets basically provide a guideline of what can be spent: they are usually short term and certainly do not extend beyond a year. Forecasts are approximations of potential future expenditures. A multiyear project probably has a budget for the first six to twelve months and a forecast for subsequent periods.

Budgets for your unit tell you how much you can spend for materials, direct and indirect labor, capital equipment, and all other related items like communication, transportation, outside meetings or conferences, education, and so on. The budget is made up of all the costs associated with your particular operation including many hidden costs. You will be charged for all the services provided by the organization. Nothing is free: you'll pay directly or indirectly but you will pay for services. You'll pay for your share of the rent, insurance, common facilities, and some share of your organization's management structure. These figures come as a shock to the new manager. Managers need to understand that nothing is *free* just because it's done by the organization. You will pay your fair share depending on the size of the unit.

Forecasts speak to the future. Questions like "What are you forecasting in subsequent years for new projects?" and "What are you forecasting for cost reduction programs, for quality improvement, for manpower needs?" create significant difficulties for the new manager. The typical response is "I've never done this before, so where do I start?" Not very many new managers demonstrate any competence in forecasting. Forecasting is looking to the future and taking a definitive position on some issue. But how did you forecast your future work as a professional? You leaned from experience. Standards are difficult to find. So, there's only one way to begin the task: involve the people in your department, manager peers, and your own manager. The final decision is your responsibility but their input is vital.

This is also an opportunity to bring your people into full partnership. Bringing all their thoughts into a pool for open discussion usually generates new opportunities. You may be the manager but you do not have all the specialized disciplinary knowledge needed and your application experience is also limited. You will generate more projects than will ever be approved so you determine the value added from each project and develop a priority list. But value added cannot be defined in financial terms only. Certain projects will be authorized whether justified financially or not, because they just need to be done. It's difficult to place a value-added figure on a customer service department but there will be a customer service department.

The forecasting process is the same whether it's for new projects, cost reduction, quality control, or manpower needs. As an example, consider forecasting the manpower needs for a project. What a dilemma: this project may take one or two years and the time of several people, and you're supposed to provide an answer? Yes, that's your job. You may not know what you're doing but you will come up with an answer for each project you recommend to your manager. This is where you as the new manager really go out on a limb. You're new so you haven't had the opportunity to develop any rules of thumb, those shortcuts that come from experience and that you might have used as a professional. So you and your staff estimate time and cost by breaking down a project into its smallest pieces and then adding them up and probably multiplying by a safety factor. Your manager may not accept this figure because it's either too high or too low. So, you're back to the proverbial drawing board either by yourself or with the assistance of your manager. If your manager believes in coaching this will present an opportunity to teach you how to make a forecast.

Forecasting your unit's requirements only requires asking and answering some very fundamental questions. What is the outcome if we invest resources in this project? What do we receive from this investment: cost savings, greater market penetration, faster turnaround on financial information, customer satisfaction, improved quality, or other results? The outcome may be measured quantitatively or qualitatively but there must be some measure of the outcome. The forecast for your unit involves adding all the costs and benefits that you propose. You have the benefit that your immediate manager and many others will scrutinize your forecast. One caution: be prepared to justify your recommendations. This may be a major part of your first appraisal as a manager.

Focusing on the Customer

Who are your customers? At one time the word *customers* referred to those who bought our products or services. Some years ago someone introduced the idea that organizations have internal customers. Product development is a customer of marketing and sales, engineering is a customer of manufacturing, all organizational functions are customers of the legal and patent departments, and the administrative functions also have their internal customers. It's unfortunate that we now refer to internal colleagues at all levels as customers. The originator of the idea of *internal customers* probably had good intentions but like so many other management ideas didn't identify the associated problems. We do not share all information or knowledge with our external customers. That same philosophy could be troublesome if people within a project or people in different organizational units do not openly share their knowledge and concerns with internal colleagues. Successful organizations depend on sharing knowledge, interests, and conflicts openly. It's too late to recognize that some pertinent information has not been communicated when the results of months of work are to be presented to a customer. Perhaps use of the word *colleagues* instead of customers is more appropriate. There's also an arms-length relationship with external customers: they are not privy to secret processes, organizational strategies, and customer archives.

With all the emphasis on customer service, reality has not matched the rhetoric. Seldom is it possible to contact someone in person. The now common automatic phone answering system telling you to press 1, followed by another message and instructions to press another number, followed by another and another, then an admonition that your call may be monitored for quality purposes, and then an extended wait for the customer service representative, hardly represents meeting the principles related to customer service. Many Web sites do not even list a telephone number. Emails regarding services are not answered promptly. The recommendations coming from some software program and transmitted by an untrained person hardly meet the minimal customer service requirements. Nevertheless that's the environment in which we work.

As a manager you may conclude that customer service does not apply unless you are specifically involved in customer service. On the contrary, most everyone is involved in customer service. As products became more complex with increased performance expectations, organizations allocated more resources to customer service. Buyers expect more than delivery of the order; they now need support. Customers need to understand the workings of the product and its capabilities and limitations. So education of the customer takes on new meaning. We have all experienced various degrees of frustration when products are delivered and simply do not work or meet requirements. So as a manager you may find the need to go into the field and meet the customer. There is nothing like face-to-face contact with a customer to resolve a problem or to gain insight into how your equipment or services are meeting the customer's needs. Managing the customer service relationship requires:

❑ Managing the buyer/seller relationship before and after delivery

❑ Keeping the customer informed if, as, and when problems occur

❑ Working with the customer to optimize the benefits to their business

❑ Observing customer's operations to determine future product needs

❑ Providing performance feedback and customer attitude after installation

Managing the Manager's Work

The five preceding activities that comprise the manager's action hat may even surprise some seasoned managers. I have found that too often managers fail to focus on these operational activities. Too often they fail to recognize the scope of their activities as managers. And then again it may not be surprising since most managers do not receive an introduction as to what it takes to be a manager. Regardless of their experiences as professionals they lack a basic understanding of the requirements for managing. Organizations have not taken the time to introduce managers to the manager's work. This lack of concern results in creating an environment that accepts mediocrity as its standard of performance.

Managers make decisions without all the facts. That's a given. A manager who waits until all the facts are documented will never make a decision. Even professionals should be aware of the 80/20 rule. If they became competent professionals before taking on management responsibilities, they should have realized that even in their own discipline all the information was never available. The 80/20 rule is very simple. Eighty percent of the information can generally be acquired in twenty percent of the time. Eighty percent of the value can be achieved with twenty percent of the effort. Reaching eighty percent of a target can be achieved with twenty percent of the resources. Decision processes are never binary. They do not include yes or no, true or false, or black or white. They usually include a "yes" or "no" with qualifications, a partially true and partially false, and not black or white but shades of gray.

Building a sustaining group presents one of the greatest challenges to managers. The history of effective organizational development is quite dismal, with few success stories. The lack of success comes from not recognizing the eight activities described in this chapter that are required to build an effective operating unit. Giving a directive from above and bringing in the latest academic or newly minted industrial gurus is bound to fail. Research clearly shows that people are at the base of all change and must be brought into the process. Restructuring the organization, repositioning those boxes on the organization chart, and contriving new slogans to energize the organization will not alter performance.

THE HIGH-ANXIETY HAT: THE MOST CHALLENGING WORK

Managers also often wear the high-anxiety hat. These tasks are performed without any joy and become a painful reminder of problems managers face. These are challenging tasks that test a manager's competence to function when faced with critical decisions. They may not occur often but they define the manager's character and involvement. Fortunately there are not too many. The following examples define the high-anxiety hat:

❑ ***Dealing with Harassment and Addiction.*** There is no doubt that you will encounter problems regarding harassment and addiction of various types. You will most likely resolve such issues with interaction from the human resource and legal departments. These become serious matters because if the wrong perceptions persist careers can be destroyed. But your role is to ask the right questions. You cannot sit on the sidelines and leave the decision to the human resource and legal people. You must actively participate. You owe it to your employees. You don't take sides. You demand that company politics not enter the discussion.

❑ ***Coping with the Death of an Employee or an Employee's Close Relative.*** What would you do if one of your team died when on an assignment in another city? Could you approach the spouse or the parents and pass on the sad news? How would you approach the immediate family? You can't just leave it up to the human resource people. This person worked with you; at the very least you have responsibility to be the messenger. You can't pass the buck to some unknown person.

❑ ***Having the Courage to Discipline.*** Most organizations have policies and procedures (P&P) related to employee disciplinary action, and the fewer the better. Interpretation and implementation of those policies is left to the manager's discretion. Those P&P's usually hinder freedom of operation. Managers need to determine the limits. But that takes a lot of courage. Disciplining for anything other than serious infractions is a waste of time and only destroys morale.

❑ ***Managing Nonperformers.*** Managing nonperformers requires coaching and monitoring for improved performance. They cannot do it all on their own. Maybe you hired this person as one of the best and brightest. You need to ask what happened. Did you have the courage to face up to the problem when it first became apparent?

❑ *Having the Courage to Dismiss a Person*. At some time you will be forced to dismiss an employee. This is painful but necessary. As long as you have given an employee the opportunity to improve and it's rejected there is no alternative. The major question is whether the employee has what it takes to perform effectively.

❑ *Being a Constructive Maverick*. As a manager you'll need to display some of those maverick characteristics—curiosity, tenacity, passion, and stick-to-itiveness. You'll need to ask the questions most people fail to ask in order to determine the future of your group. Just think how many unpopular positions over the centuries have changed our way of thinking. We can begin with Copernicus, go on with Galileo, and list many other renegades of traditional thought. The new will always be suspect. Being the constructive maverick is not for everyone. It takes a lot of courage to go against the flow.

❑ *Bootlegging Resources*. At 3M, one of the most innovative organizations in the world, the *bootlegging of resources* has been enshrined. Bootleg the resources you need to prove a principle or to explore what would never be officially sanctioned. You beg or borrow resources to prove a concept. This does not imply doing anything unethical or illegal. As a manager, you may not be able to sanction an action, but you can defend it if it becomes necessary. Your role as manager is to assist your colleagues in finding those resources.

❑ *Admitting Mistakes.* Admitting mistakes is not the most pleasant task for any of us. But admit them when they happen. You can't cover them up without severe consequences to your reputation. You're going to make some mistakes and some of them may seem dumb to certain individuals. It takes courage to admit that you were wrong. Keep in mind that a mistake to one person may be a source of future opportunities for another person. Today's mistake may be tomorrow's innovation. Mistakes determine progress; learn from them. They're absolutely necessary.

THE BUSINESS HAT: WHERE IT ALL COMES TOGETHER

As a professional in some discipline your perspective of the business of the organization was limited. You had knowledge of the purposes and objectives of your group but limited knowledge of the organization. As long as the organization was meeting its objectives there was not much reason to go beyond the interests of your group. Your manager filled you in on what was necessary. As a specialist you probably didn't take an interest in the decisions of upper management unless those decisions affected your working conditions in some way. Only a small percentage of professionals even know the names and contributions of upper management.

Academia, government, industry, and not-for-profit organizations are all involved in some form of business; I use the word *business* in its broadest sense. Each expects a result from the investment of its resources. Each has or should have defined purposes, objectives, and strategies to reach its objectives. The business of academia is to educate. The business of government at all levels is to provide the social infrastructure. The business of industry is to provide the products and services that meet society's needs. The business of not-for-profit organizations is to provide those social services that enhance the human condition.

As a new appointee to a management position you will become more closely allied with the *business* of the organization. The work and actions and decisions taken in your unit will impact other organizational units. You are no longer an island unto yourself. As a manager your responsibility is to open the doors to those other silos and explore their content. Your future and that of your unit depend on discovering what's in those silos. You feed those other silos and they in turn feed you. As a manager you determine the feeding schedule. Opening those silo doors will be met with various kinds of resistance. You can't assume that everyone will cooperate. As a matter of fact, you need to ready yourself for a hard sell. The current managers built these silos and have become comfortable. You're messing with the comfort zone.

Becoming part of the management team adds additional responsibilities beyond managing the activities of your unit. The six hats previously discussed focused on responsibilities to your unit. As a manager you may be asked to participate in discussions with other organizational units where your professional competence is required. Your announcement immediately gave you visibility that you did not have before. You will also be asked to participate in activities totally unrelated to your unit responsibilities. These may include a position on some human resource committee; a task force to search for new organizational opportunities; a task force to reduce paperwork; a task force to deal with developing new strategies; a task force to change the project approval process; and any number of other committees or task forces that deal with issues related to the total organization. Don't scoff at such assignments because they detract from the work related to your unit. But how you participate in these activities gives you an opportunity to set the pace and gain credibility with senior managers from other organizational units. Your level of participation will determine your future.

Moving your unit forward requires exposure to upper management. You can't hide in the closet. Your successes and failures will be visible. Upper management will know what you're doing and how your activities affect the bottom line regardless of how that bottom line is measured. To make a business-like impression on upper management you need to know who these people are and where they're coming from. You need to understand something about how they wish to interact with others. Some may want the whole story; others may just want the summary. Some may want to go into the details, others may only ask what it does for the organization. You're on center stage and building a reputation. Your actions are building a track record that determines your future in management. Upper management will begin to develop confidence in you as a person and your ability to manage. You're part of management, so find a way to participate. But know what you're talking about. A little study of the issue gives you the upper hand.

The process of building confidence does not imply accepting everything that upper management presents as gospel. But how you react and interact does make a difference. Thoughtful comments will usually be accepted. Upper management often institutes various programs to which you and your colleagues may object and your concerns should be noted. However, merely criticizing a program doesn't add any benefit and is a waste of time and effort. Identifying and communicating the problems that may occur by instituting the program provides a more thoughtful approach as long as the new approach does not appear to be self-serving. Making an alternative proposal also provides an opportunity to counter any negative impact on your unit but may require too much effort for the expected benefits. So, learn to pick your battles where they provide the most benefit. Stick to the facts regardless of where they take you.

You may complain about the role of politics in the decision-making process. Politics is not a dirty word unless the politics become dirty; character assassination has no place in any organizational setting, becoming personal rather than factual cannot be sanctioned, distortion of information cannot be tolerated, and lying requires serious corrective action. What most people refer to as politics involves what appears to be favoritism. People develop relationships and those relationships often span a lifetime; those relations are often viewed as political. As a young manager you will be very quickly accused of playing politics when you recommend or not recommend someone for a particular position or approve or disapprove a new project. Chances are that you will make those decisions because you choose to select a known quantity. If you have to make a choice between two people for a particular position and both have comparable competencies across the board and the only difference is that at one time you worked with one of the people, which one will you choose? You will probably choose the known quantity. Successful careers require support from others. You can't do it alone on the strength of your ideas, your commitment, and your character. But don't play the destructive dirty politics game.

SUMMARY

Managers must change among these seven hats whenever required. Each requires a different approach depending on the issues under consideration. Balancing the use of these seven hats challenges not only the new but also the experienced manager.

❑ *The Administration Hat*: Managing the nuts and bolts of the administrative routines can be delegated and should not dominate the manager's focus. Administration is an important function but by itself does not add value. It detracts from performance when not managed effectively and efficiently.

❑ **The Direction Hat**: Managers provide direction by teaching, coaching, promoting, innovating, working, and being responsive to the needs of the organization and its people. Managers build a proactive organization by maximizing the participation of available talent and providing the competencies for the future.

❑ **The Leadership Hat**: Leadership must be kept in perspective at the levels; it is not corporate leadership, and that's why I've referred to it as *taking the lead*. You become the leader by being the pathfinder, the visionary, and the coalition builder, and by providing opportunities for your professional staff to meet the organization's objectives and their personal career objectives.

❑ **The People Hat**: People are the most important asset and must be treated as the most important asset. Managers without some minimal understanding of human behavior create their own problems. People are unique so treat them accordingly. What may motivate one may not motivate another. One dictum: treat everyone with respect.

❑ **The Action Hat**: The action hat involves developing and understanding the workload; knowing the people and their competencies and limitations; budgeting and forecasting the need for resources; focusing on the needs of internal (I prefer using the term "colleagues" or "partners" for internal contacts) and external customers; and managing the manager's work.

❑ **The High-Anxiety Hat**: Managers face situations that test their moral and philosophical grounding, those challenging tasks that deal with serious people problems that cannot be avoided. Delaying these decisions creates a disquieting environment that generates frustration and takes up valuable time.

❑ **The Business Hat**: You are part of the organization's management so now is the time to take on those management responsibilities. Although your primary concerns relate to your unit, you now have a further responsibility to take into account the impact that your decisions have on other organizational units.

Making the Critical People Decisions

The next step on this journey toward taking on a managing responsibility involves dealing with the people issues. The activities on the continuum from hiring to retirement or termination test the manager's competence and credibility. As a newly minted manager you may not be concerned about the retirement of your people, but keep in mind that you will play a role in their career development that will affect their retirement. Initially you will probably inherit staff from the previous manager. The process of building a team involves using the inherited talent plus making certain changes. These changes may include adding employees or perhaps transferring some to other departments. Your success as a manager depends on how well you build, educate, position, coach, and evaluate your people. The following nine issues require your careful consideration as you manage the activities of your department:

1. Selecting staff
2. Building careers
3. Educating and training
4. Enhancing career opportunities
5. Coaching
6. Reviewing performance
7. Paying for performance
8. Managing harassment, discrimination, and termination
9. Dealing with the human resources department

SELECTING STAFF FOR THE ORGANIZATIONAL UNIT

Selecting staff involves working with the current assigned staff and hiring additional personnel. As a newly assigned manager you inherit a staff. Initially, as noted in Chapter 2, you need to determine each individual's competencies and determine how those competencies integrate into your department's capabilities. You are now faced with hiring new people. What are the guidelines?

Staffing your department may be quite different from others. Research departments require people that will differ markedly from operations or administrative departments. A department staffed with people involved in routine activities will be quite different from the one focused on innovation. Staffing must be based on needs. I have heard many HR people claim, "we hire only the top 10 percent of the class." That may be a justified goal as long as you need the top ten percent of the class. But hiring the right people depends on more than grade-point average. High grade-point average without drive, energy, and the ability to work with others doesn't make the grade today. There is little demand for secluded specialists or thinkers of great thoughts.

There are differences in recruiting a college graduate with a baccalaureate degree, a graduate with an advanced degree, and an experienced professional. The typical college recruiting program in large organizations involves a call for some number of people in various disciplines. The emphasis is placed on the academic record, any related outside activities, and general screening of personal traits. The HR people and occasionally some discipline-related people make the initial screening at the university campus. They later circulate the applications with their comments within the organization to the hiring managers to determine the level of interest in particular candidates. The managers sign up to interview the candidates of interest, and HR extends the invitation for an interview at some appropriate location. The process concludes with an offer of employment or a rejection and will vary depending on the organization and its relations with the various universities. In smaller organizations the process is less formal and often involves a personal call to a professor with whom the manager may have a business or social relationship.

Hiring people with advanced degrees or experience becomes more personal and is often initiated by the hiring manager. The process involves developing a detailed job description that includes the required educational background, specific disciplinary interest, and a past history of personal contributions at other organizations. The job description focuses on specific questions, such as: What do you want this person to do? What does the work involve? What knowledge, skills, attitudes, personal characteristics, and experiences does the applicant bring to the company?

When there's a position to be filled that has certain very specific requirements, it's not enough to say we need an organic chemist or a computer scientist or a human behavior specialist or a statistician with a Ph.D. or some number of years of experience. When it involves hiring a Ph.D., the candidate's research must somehow be linked to the organization's needs. When it involves hiring a person with experience, that experience must also be somehow linked to the organization's needs. The importance of a well-defined job description cannot be overemphasized, but the description must also be realistic. Too many people with advanced degrees and experience somehow fail to meet expectations.

When you find a candidate who meets the requirements of the job description, make an offer. Managers too often find a candidate who meets the job requirements but then continue the interview process. What a waste of time. My comment to these managers is to either hire the person or change the job description. If the candidate meets the requirements, why vacillate? If you say that the person you interviewed "meets all the requirements, but I might find someone better," then evidently the candidate does not really meet the requirements.

The key to hiring the right people depends on the manager who conducts the interview process. While the job description is important and can guide the direction of the interview, the process involves going beyond the written word. What do you want to learn about the candidate? You have obviously been interviewed in your years of experience as a professional; what did you learn from those interviews? They should have taught you a great deal about the process and the interviewers.

Were these interviews social chitchat or did the interviewer get down to a nuts and bolts kind of discussion about the requirements and your ability to meet the requirements? Did the interviewer ask you to discuss the specifics of your contributions with other organizations and focus on your track record? Did the interviewer go beyond what was on the employment application? Did the interviewer ask the hard questions in relation to your ability to travel, to relocate to another city or take a foreign assignment, to put in the overtime when necessary, to work on multiple projects, and your ability to not only accept change but to pursue it? If you've ever gone through a rigorous interview process as a professional in your discipline you should have no difficulty framing your questions in such a way as to find out what this candidate is capable of doing.

What are some approaches to discovering a candidate's competencies, attitudes, and characteristics? At the undergraduate or semiprofessional level, academic credentials coupled with other interests and experience provide about the only possibilities to evaluate the candidate. The academic credentials are a given and class standing cannot be disputed. But that academic standing must fit the job requirements. Managers too often minimize the *other interests and experience* category. Exploration of these other interests and experience—even if that experience consists entirely of part-time jobs held while going to school—provides a great deal of information about the candidate's attitudes and characteristics. They often demonstrate personal initiative, ability to work not just with others but also alone if necessary, the ability to both accept and influence change, the ability to communicate at all levels, and the ability to lead.

For hiring candidates with advanced degrees or with prior directly related job experience, I have used two approaches successfully:

1. Ask the candidate to give a presentation to a select group of people on a related topic. The candidate may be asked to give an impromptu presentation of his or her field of interest.

2. Pose a problem and ask how the candidate might approach the problem. This approach gives you information about what the candidate may have contributed personally in previous jobs. It is necessary to sort out the individual's contribution from the team's contribution. You are not hiring the rest of the team.

What are you as the manager going to tell the candidate about the department? The candidate has probably received the public relations package about the organization but how will you supplement that with information about your own and related departments? Will you provide an opportunity for the candidate to speak to people in your group to gain their impressions of the real world? Will you give the candidate a tour of the department and related areas? Will you fully explain the type of work that is performed by the department; actually go through some typical projects but maintaining confidentiality where necessary? Will you give the candidate some idea of what the first work assignments might be? The interview process is a two-way street; you must understand the strengths and limitations of the candidate and the candidate must leave with a full and realistic understanding of the job requirements and possible assignments.

BUILDING CAREERS

As a manager you actively participate in career building: providing opportunities to those assigned to you to develop current and future competencies and to take on greater responsibilities in developing the organization's future. You should quickly recognize that experience builds careers and lack of experience destroys careers. You will find people who have had ten years of experience in ten years of work and others who have had one year of experience ten times. There is a significant difference in these two career paths. Remaining in the same position and doing the same work in the same way for many years seldom creates the necessary challenges for developing a successful career. Unfortunately too many employees find themselves in this position because their managers prefer to react to circumstances rather than take a proactive position.

Successful careers are built on accepting new challenges that span a continuum from minor to major. What may be a minor challenge to one person may be a major challenge to another. However, not all employees can accept a major challenge. The challenge must somehow correlate with the ability and the desire of the individual to accept change. Level of education is not the issue. Attitudes and personal characteristics of the individual determine the desire to accept a challenge. While not every person can accept a major challenge, all must accept some appropriate level to justify their existence in the organization. If you avoid challenging employees to improve their performance, you will eventually face the prospect of terminating some of these employees.

Building the careers of assigned or newly hired people does not fall solely on your shoulders. The individual must eventually take responsibility, but the manager plays a role in directing that career. If you fail to act in a timely manner with an employee who is not meeting expectations and recognize that his or her career has stalled because of some set of circumstances, then you're not performing your responsibility as a manager. Too often managers give an employee too much time to correct the situation and in the process exacerbate the situation. You deal with such situations through extensive communication with the employee and an agreement of some kind of probationary period during which the individual will have an opportunity to correct the situation but with your guidance. If as an example you hired a new person and after a year or more the person does not meet performance targets, you need to look at your past actions and see where you dropped the ball. What was your role in this employee's failure? Indifference on your part? Lack of direct communication regarding performance? What was the cause? There must be an answer.

EDUCATING AND TRAINING

Lifelong learning begins on graduation day. Four years of education hardly prepares us for a lifetime career in any discipline. There is a significant difference between a career and a job. As a young manager I considered education and training as my responsibility. I almost forced people, but not quite, to continue their education in some form and on some topic of interest to them. I used operational meetings to educate the staff. As our world continues to become more complex, lifelong learning becomes doubly important.

HR departments are generally given the responsibility for education and training, but managers cannot abdicate the responsibility for providing proper educational opportunities. If HR has programs that meet your group's needs, take advantage of them but only after careful evaluation. My major concerns about HR recommendations relate to courses that focus on creativity, team building, performance management, leadership, and that whole class of programs that deal with the soft skills—the interpersonal skills. These courses are absolutely vital but must address real problems with substance. Everyone will not be creative. Everyone will not be a leader. The normal distribution curve will apply. Some small percentage of the staff will drive the group. Too many of these courses teach these interpersonal skills as though the manager lives in a rose garden and only needs to smell the roses.

Education and training that's directed toward the professions requires the manager's scrutiny for relevance to current as well as future organizational needs. Most HR people, unless they have been transplanted from some professional group to HR, are not familiar with the requirements of a particular discipline and cannot possibly make reliable recommendations. They can do a search at the request of the manager and then allow the manager to make the decision. I suggest that you use the HR department to do the search for programs that respond to your department's educational needs, but the final decision lies with you.

Organizations spend billions of dollars annually for education and training. They fund all types of education in many different disciplines and even extend learning opportunities in various types of MBA courses related to technology, marketing, and manufacturing. They also fund internal programs that relate solely to the continued operation of the organization. However, the number of people who invest their personal funds in furthering their work-related education doesn't appear anywhere in the statistics; as an executive, consultant, and educator I seldom encountered an individual who invested personal funds in work-related education and training.

So much for lifelong learning. So what do you do as a newly appointed manager?

Learning must emphasize the future. Building a proactive and energetic department that not only serves the present but also anticipates future needs requires that education and training have a high priority. Some of that learning comes from experience as a result of undertaking new challenges and exposure to new ideas, but some formal learning allows the individual to get a head start. As a professional you probably had some number of designated hours allocated for education; forty hours per year seems to be the norm except for special situations, and this is usually verified at the time of appraisal. Forty hours is hardly sufficient to keep abreast of discipline changes or expand to new disciplines unless supplemented with work challenges and stretch targets.

Much of the investment in education and training has little impact on the organization's results. The difficulty with most education and training programs is that they are not linked to current or future work. Managers often state that they don't know what's on the horizon. If they did their job of managing they would keep abreast of the latest in their field through the various professional organizations that serve their field of interest.

While learning is important, it is also often necessary to *unlearn* what has been learned in the past. This is particularly true in relationship to work methods, processes, and methods of thinking. Unlearning work methods and processes should not present a problem. Some form of logic can be demonstrated to make methods or process changes. But some people will always resist change regardless of the magnitude.

Unlearning old thinking methods does create a problem for many people. This is a difficult transition to make for many specialists. As an example, throughout this book I stress the need to focus on the impact of any work effort on the total system rather than just the limited piece of the individual's concern. To tear down all those independent silos requires a lot of unlearning. To attempt to capitalize on the application of digital technology requires unlearning old methods. As communications go more toward the electronic a great deal of unlearning and learning must take place. As a paradigm shift takes place old ways must be discarded and new ways implemented. Asking people to think in terms of the impact of their effort on the system is a paradigm shift. What you do in your sandbox must be based on the needs of all those other sandboxes.

You have many resources for educating your staff. Education is available at universities with unlimited specialties, community colleges, industrial training organizations, professional organizations, and now Web-based learning can provide learning in the family living room. People learn differently. Some people make progress in their profession without any formal education and training because of the nature of their work; these are people who work on the cutting edge of their profession. If you and your staff are working on the leading edge you won't have to spend much time and effort benchmarking your efforts against others. You are the benchmark. Some people need formal courses while others learn more by spending a half-day in the library reading related books or scanning the latest related journals published by professional organizations. Lifelong learning is not going to go away. But the benefit from investing in education and training must be measured. Those workshops on creativity that you authorized for your key people really didn't provide any benefit. Don't expect much from any workshop regardless of the presenter's credentials unless followed up with specific opportunities for implementation.

ENHANCING CAREER OPPORTUNITIES

Why is proper placement such an important issue? Are you placing your people in positions that provide for career growth? Are your people working at or above their level of competence? Does the organization's culture support leading edge thinking in all disciplines or is it just satisfied in meeting its competition? Do you energize your employees *to go for the gold*? Why do some of your best and brightest fail to meet expectations? These questions need to be considered seriously as you take over the managing of your department. You're in the process of building an effective department not only for today but also for the future. The organization has a major investment in your staff and thus part of your responsibility is to make sure that it continues to provide the competencies now and in the future.

While there are no simple answers to these concerns and questions, we do know that unless managers raise expectations people have a tendency to become comfortable and lose interest, and then their energy tends to wane. Unless there is a continual emphasis on personal improvement, performance will decrease. Group performance will decline unless each manager strives to place people in positions that allow for growth. Of course the expectations need to be in line with the available resources and the organization's objectives. The process begins by providing specific assignments for growth to people who have the basic competence but need to acquire additional knowledge and experience to be professionally fit for the future's more challenging assignments.

Managers enhance career growth by providing new opportunities. Every new opportunity affords new experiences. In today's world, where so much emphasis is placed on specialization, it becomes even more important to provide new opportunities in related disciplines or subdisciplines. Segmentation of disciplines and overspecialization in a subdiscipline eventually leads to obsolescence, and the knowledge and expertise of that subdiscipline are no longer required. The time to prevent obsolescence begins long before it occurs, which is one more of your responsibilities as the manager.

We all begin our careers in some particular discipline. As we progressed in that discipline to become professionals we encountered many other disciplines that played a major role in our performance and that of the organization. During that period we should have learned something not only about the needs of those other disciplines but also how to make the necessary accommodations. As an example, marketing and product development groups continually find themselves in contentious relationships and too often to the detriment of the organization. Marketers and engineers do not think the same way. Engineers want specifics, marketers want flexibility. Marketers complain about the engineers' obstinacy in disregarding their marketing requirements; engineers complain that marketing can never define the product requirements. Both groups are right and both groups are wrong.

From the engineers' point of view, marketing comes to them with the customers' wants or needs, with limited information to justify assigning the resources and with impossible delivery dates. Marketing seldom meets with the people who would actually be using the new product. When asked for evidence of the need and the specifics, they have little to present. Marketing can seldom make sales forecasts on new products or services with sufficient accuracy for the engineers; they're either high or low but seldom right. 3M's Post-it Notes provide an excellent example; marketing initially didn't think the product had any possibilities.

From the marketers' point of view, engineers often try to introduce more bells and whistles than marketing suggests. They refuse to change the scope of the project once it has been finalized. Engineers want to use the latest technologies when the latest technologies really provide no short- or long-term benefit. Engineers want too many details and get caught up in the minutiae and forget about the big picture.

So how do you bring these marketers and engineers or any other two or more groups together to resolve their differences and reduce the countless hours of misplaced effort? As a rule, marketers know little if anything about engineering and engineers know little or nothing about marketing. An exchange of positions would be a possible solution but would most likely end with disastrous consequences for the organization. In my career I have been on both sides of this divide. The solution is simple. Start bringing people together from different functions. In this case, send the engineers out in the field with the marketers to gain first-hand knowledge from the customers. In many situations engineers can ask the right questions and gain insight into the use of the new product or suggest modification to a current product. Let the marketers spend some time with the engineers in developing the conceptual models of the new product. They need not be technically competent. They only need to be able to translate the customers' needs and their thoughts to the engineers.

Bringing marketing and engineering together begins with selecting the two people who have the best chance of demonstrating what can be accomplished when people work toward a common goal. You don't necessarily need your best marketer or best engineer. Select the people who have some people skills and can find a common interest. As a manager you have a responsibility to bring those isolated silos together. Will it take time? Yes. Will it be difficult? Probably. But it's worth a try.

There is another approach if the organization's top management believes in multidisciplinary involvement. As a young engineer I was expected to attend several of the organization's trade shows and do booth duty and face the satisfied and unsatisfied customers just as my counterparts in marketing and sales were doing. This gave me face-to-face contact with people who used the product and told me in no uncertain terms what they liked and disliked about it and the organization. What an educational experience. What an audience from which to get new ideas about meeting customer needs and developing a network for providing feedback.

This example basically says to let each person walk in the other's shoes to gain some idea of the problems. They really don't have to walk very far. Give them an opportunity to understand the limitations and restrictions under which each works. Don't try to make engineers out of marketers and marketers out of engineers, just focus them on getting an understanding of each other's requirements.

While this example uses the introduction of a new product in an industrial setting, the same principles apply to all activities in academia, government, and other not-for-profit organizations. The academic community and government, like industry, are made up of independent silos called departments that are essentially autonomous. Each department has its own agenda. Occasionally groups will join forces. Academic departments operate independently with little if any concern for the greater system called the university. Government agencies seldom cooperate in joint ventures that would provide improved services or reduce costs. Attempting to convince a group of academicians to focus on a problem from a system perspective rarely occurs. Many governmental decisions focus on some single issue and totally disregard the impact on other entities. The not-for-profit organizations crosscut many different interests and operate within their own independent silos; fund raising, operations, future directions, and so on.

COACHING

Too often, when we speak about coaching we invoke the sports model as our guide—those professional sports coaches who pace the sidelines or the bull pens with their assistants at their side calling the next plays, cursing the players and the umpires, muttering some obscenities, and raging at an umpire's decision that affects them adversely. This model does not apply to coaching the many professional and semiprofessionals who make up today's workforce.

Phillip B. Crosby,[1] in *Quality is Free*, wrote that "Quality was ballet, not hockey." He used the phrase to indicate that quality required unblinking dedication, patience, and time and that no single piece of information would clarify or resolve a quality problem. Coaching professionals is more like learning ballet; practice, practice, and more practice supported by dedication, discipline, patience, and understanding. The orchestra conductor brings out the best in each musician so that the final product achieves its share of bravos. In essence the conductor is the coach.

Coaching can relate to the professional's discipline, related skills, attitudes, career issues, personnel problems, and future opportunities. As coach you provide guidance in developing interpersonal, operational, and administrative skills; those skills that are practiced in your particular organizational context. You also may be required to resolve problems related to nonperformance or underperformance. Your role as coach does not include providing the best answer. Your goal is to challenge the thinking processes, to ask the tough questions, to put the person or group on the right track without imposing your own prejudices. Coaching should be an exercise in self-discovery for individuals or groups. However, from your position as the manager, the coaching must eventually resolve the issue.

Improving performance through coaching requires face-to-face interaction; it can be done either individually or in small groups. It requires absolute integrity and open communication on the part of all participants in a nonthreatening environment. It should take place in relation to some specific work-related activity rather than some abstract and unreal scenario. You need to avoid playing the role of the psychologist. Leave those issues to the appropriate human resource specialist. You are not the father confessor to resolve everyone's personal problems.

REVIEWING PERFORMANCE

Upper management through its human resource professionals places a great deal of emphasis on performance appraisals. Those appraisals involve both individual and group appraisals. That emphasis usually originates with the CEO. But HR professionals tend to emphasize qualities that may not necessarily meet your requirements. You may hear suggestions that you can't rate a person below some level. Rating a person above his or her performance level in order to motivate only creates future problems. You may also hear that your best performers are too aggressive. Obviously aggressiveness that destroys team cooperation must in some way be checked but in twenty-first-century America we could probably use a little more of what I refer to as polite and respectful aggressiveness.

You may be counseled to treat everyone equally but keep in mind that we attribute uniqueness to all people and that uniqueness must be accommodated. You may be criticized for setting your performance targets too high. You may control the work of one individual more closely than another. You may allow more freedom to those who can manage it. The point is that you make these decisions. You set performance standards. You decide when aggressiveness becomes counterproductive. You integrate the uniqueness of your people into a competent working group.

Performance reviews present a major stumbling block to organizational development. Managers dread them except when the review is positive. Employees find some shortcomings whether the review is positive or negative. The format changes every three or four years, the process becomes more complex, it requires more time, and then all those records go into the organization's archives only to be released when some legal issue becomes apparent. The results of all those good intentions are difficult to quantify during the following year's evaluation. Evaluating performance is absolutely essential but requires information that generally lacks the specifics related to actual accomplishments.

Evaluating performance need not be an unpleasant task. In my first year of employment after receiving a university degree I asked my manager whether there was a formal appraisal system in the company. His reply was that I "should keep in mind that every time we meet you're being appraised." We did have a formal performance review and it began by my manager opening a folder with many slips of paper, plus a summary of those slips of paper, and a one-page written report on my performance. While the evaluation was very positive, I was struck by the amount of information he had about my year's performance. That was my first formal evaluation and I have followed that procedure throughout my many years in management.

Unfortunately, most managers often do not have sufficient documented information to make an intelligent assessment of an employee's performance. The annual or semiannual employee appraisal may be an anachronism in today's economy. Can you as a manager wait six months to provide feedback on an employee's performance? As my first manager noted, *keep in mind that every time we meet you're being appraised*, and provide the feedback now. Also place a note in the file. Disagreements usually arise because of a lack of documentation.

Performance evaluation begins long before the day scheduled for the evaluation. It begins the day after the last evaluation. It begins with establishing some short- and long-term objectives depending on the organization's workload. Management by objectives (MBO) receives a great deal of bad press, but how can you expect people to meet performance requirements without setting goals and objectives? MBO worked until it became a tool of the human resource department that transformed it into a time-consuming paper mill; instead of focusing on performance it focused on filling out forms.

Practical application of MBO has nothing to do with the HR department. MBO is an agreement between the employee and his or her manager. It is a statement of agreed-upon expectations. We don't need a formal contract to describe the employee's expectations. The critical issue that is too often lost is that you as the manager are part of the objective. Yes, you are part of the objective. You cannot be in absentia and then criticize the employee for nonperformance. You have close contact with your employees, so you shouldn't wait until the date of delivery to know whether the work effort will meet the requirements.

Evaluating the performance of the group includes evaluating individual performance. The performance of each group member might meet expectations but that does not guarantee meeting the organization's expectations. The group could also meet expectations while some members of the group may not have met their expectations. Each department has a particular mission to fulfill. Measuring the performance against that mission becomes somewhat problematic. It's not possible to just add up all the individual levels of accomplishments and attribute them to the group.

We know that less than ten percent of projects meet their specifications, are completed on time, and meet the original cost estimates. At the same time the majority of employees have been evaluated as either meeting or exceeding requirements. There is clearly a disconnect here. There are many reasons for not meeting these three requirements, and the majority stem from not diligently doing what I've referred to as the up-front work: developing and reaching agreement on a comprehensive and understandable work statement; assigning people with the right mix of skills and competencies; developing the work plan; engaging in the follow-up of the work plan; and monitoring the execution of the many details. These are all straightforward management activities that on the surface are very simple and mundane activities but are seldom given due attention. As a manager you need to work with your employees and other managers to develop the yardstick by which performance will be measured.

PAYING FOR PERFORMANCE

Maintaining equitable salaries within an organization poses many challenges. Salary schedules are usually dictated from the top of the organization, but if you take the initiative to fight for what your department needs you can win. It depends on your approach. For all practical purposes most organizations follow some form of automatic progression system such as a general percentage increase across the board. Some modify the process and differentiate the percentage increases depending on the person's performance rating. A person receiving an "A" rating will receive a slightly higher percentage than the person rated a "B" and so on. In practice this means that there is usually not much differentiation in salary increases.

Merit pay becomes problematic since an additional one or two percent hardly compensates for that extra effort put forth by some people. HR people prefer to align their pay schedules according to some predetermined plan that treats everyone the same. Although compensation is not a long-term motivator, some form of additional compensation must be provided for those who make a significant contribution.

As a manager you need to pursue the right to allocate increases based on the amount allocated to your group. Is this a difficult task? Yes. While HR experts will argue that money is not the major factor for instilling dedication, it is still a factor. You can't build an excellent team by dividing the financial pot equally across all employees. Most teams will have a distribution of people; some will be super-dedicated, some will give you a day's work and no more, some will make only marginal value-added contributions, and then there will be some that may not deserve to be kept on the team. Linking compensation to performance provides the best approach to recognizing this reality.

There was a time when pay for performance could be implemented easily: compensation packages were confidential. Many employees now know just about what everyone in their department is being paid. Employees speak about their salaries openly. Resolve any conflicts with the facts. Keep in mind though that the people in your department need to fully understand your priorities and what you consider value-adding contributions.

MANAGING HARASSMENT, DISCRIMINATION, AND TERMINATION

Most organizations will have strict policies and procedures regarding harassment, discrimination, and termination. You may inherit these issues from the previous manager, but hopefully you will not be forced to face them immediately. The legal counsel will most likely handle the harassment and discrimination issues. Your involvement cannot go beyond impartially protecting the rights of your employees. You will provide any information relative to the charges as requested but will not generally enter into the decision process. Legal difficulties that arise as a result of a termination can be significantly reduced if adequate performance records are maintained.

Terminating an employee is probably one of the most traumatic experiences for any manager, regardless of their amount of experience. Whether that termination is related to some major infraction of organizational policy or human behavior, lack of competence, major mistake in judgment, dissolution of a department, or organization-wide downsizing at the direction of upper management, the impact is essentially the same. You may look forward to the day when you can terminate a particular individual but the day of judgment arrives and reality restarts the thought processes. You're terminating a person with whom you've been working with for perhaps many years. You may have put forth a great deal of effort in coaching the person to be a productive employee. You know their family. But this is not the time to rationalize the decision to terminate. Once you have made that decision you have no alternative but to follow through. One caution: make sure you have provided opportunities for improvement and base your decision on undisputable facts.

Most managers do not pay sufficient attention to employees whose performance drops below expectations. A comprehensive plan to improve performance, an accurate documented response to the plan by the employee, defined opportunities for improvement, close follow-up, an agreed-upon timetable, and close communication determine the level of difficulties that lie ahead. You can't rate an employee's performance as satisfactory or better for years and then terminate because of lack of performance for a short time. If the previous manager bequeathed to you such problems you have no alternative but to develop a plan for improving performance.

DEALING WITH THE HUMAN RESOURCE DEPARTMENT

In recent years HR departments have played a more aggressive role in dealing with people issues from hiring to promoting to terminating. As organizations grew in size, top management began to depend more and more on them for guidance in employee-related decisions. In many situations line managers lost control of the employee issues that affect their performance. Managers cannot allow themselves to be dominated by HR departments. This does not suggest that HR staff should be disregarded, but it does suggest that managers must look out for the good of their employees and their department.

You probably came to this management position from years of experience as a competent professional and were aware of HR activities during that tenure. You should have some understanding of the influence HR had on your manager. You probably are aware of some of his or her frustrations in dealing with HR policies and recommendations. From my experience I have found some exceedingly competent HR people in all areas. I have also found those who only bring the HR recommendations and contribute little if anything to the process. One of the easiest ways to resolve most conflicts with HR is to have a close relationship with someone you respect in HR and who speaks openly with you about any problems. This person can often be the one who recruited you, providing you've kept up the relationship after being hired. You need to choose your battles carefully and demonstrate with facts any deviations from basic HR policies and requirements. There will be times when HR will make the decision and you have no alternative but to comply.

SUMMARY

❑ Organizational success depends on integrating competencies with workload requirements not only to meet present but also future requirements. The future is now, and the time to develop those new competencies is before they are required. You may have heard the statement that we accomplish great things with average people. But keep in mind somewhere in that group of average people live some exceptional people who drive the organization.

❑ Staffing presents the greatest problems for the new manager and also the greatest opportunities. You need the appropriate individual talents that can be brought together and function as a unit.

❑ As a manager you either build or destroy careers. Standing still is really going backward in a competitive world. That's an awesome responsibility.

❑ Lifelong learning requires dedication and causes the least difficulties when people are given stretch targets that force them to focus on the leading edge in their discipline. Opportunities need to be provided for education and training that extend beyond one's immediate discipline. Such efforts not only enhance career growth but also provide significant benefits, especially in this age of overspecialization.

❑ Coaching involves more than making suggestions. It involves a relationship where performance and nonperformance can be approached objectively. Coaching involves bringing the best out in each employee.

❑ Performance reviews are one of those necessary evils that, if performed with diligence, provide a significant benefit to the individual and the organization. If they are done solely to fulfill some organizational requirement, they only waste time.

❑ Bringing everyone down to the lowest common denominator doesn't provide much incentive to go above and beyond what might be expected. Those who go the extra mile need to be compensated accordingly.

❑ Issues related to harassment, discrimination, and termination now require specialists in those fields to arrive at just solutions. Your input will be required but the specialists will make the decisions.

❑ Learn to use the resources of the HR department but recognize that you are the one who should make the decisions.

NOTE

1. Philip B. Crosby, *Quality Is Free* (New York: New American Library, 1979), p. 13.

CHAPTER 4

Managing Individual and Team Relationships

You now have some understanding of the people issue. You are responsible for developing a high-energy team that meets its commitments. You will also be called upon to function as a team member or leader for some organizational activities outside your own department. Building a team cannot be done at the expense of the individual contributor and vice versa, however.

In recent years much discussion has taken place and much has been written about teams. We know we need teams to meet organizational objectives, but teams are only the means for integrating the value added from individual contributors. Using teams involves managing relationships among individuals who come from different disciplines, with different experiences, and with different agendas. Teams are composed of people who span the continuum from the proactive to the inactive. Team members bring all the human baggage that each of us carries: our opinions, our prejudices, our personal characteristics, our attitudes, and our approach to dealing with colleagues at all levels in the organization.

We know that ideas and concepts come from individuals, although they are often triggered through dialogue with team members. One person eventually articulates an idea or concept that has been looked at from many different perspectives. So while teams are vital, the individual contributors play a significant role in team performance. The manager builds the value-adding team by:

- ❏ Defining "team"
- ❏ Setting the direction and style
- ❏ Building the team
- ❏ Learning from research
- ❏ Asking the questions and getting the answers
- ❏ Defining the role of the individual
- ❏ Using teams effectively
- ❏ Pursuing excellence
- ❏ Making diversity work
- ❏ Motivating the team
- ❏ Promoting self-managed teams

DEFINING "TEAM"

Allan Cox in *The Homework Beyond Teamwork*[1] provides a comprehensive description of the value-adding team:

> The value-adding team is a collective state of mind where ideas are food and puzzlements are challenges. It is where conflict is positive because it is out in the open. Responsiveness is paramount. Whether established department or ad hoc, the *team is a thinking organism* where problems are named, assumptions challenged, alternatives generated, con-

sequences assessed, priorities set, admissions made, competitors evaluated, missions validated, goals tested, hopes ventured, fears anticipated, successes expected, vulnerabilities expressed, contributions praised, absurdities tolerated, withdrawals noticed, victories celebrated, and defeats overcome. Finally it is where decisions are backed when the boss says yes or no to a particular option.

This description does not specify or validate any particular team structure. My years of experience have convinced me that team structure is of little importance; if the right people are available, structure really doesn't matter too much; without the right people, no organizational structure will produce the expected results. Every team requires some level of structure if for no other reason than to communicate with other departments. Members of the team cannot go in whatever directions they choose, because there are others depending on their timely performance. There must be a focus on the organization's objectives.

SETTING THE DIRECTION AND STYLE

Managers set the direction and style for the department. They determine the direction and how to travel the path toward meeting the department's objectives. As a young manager I quickly discovered that when dealing with people issues, the shortest distance between the problem and the answer was not a straight line. We're not dealing with human clones. We're working with people who display all kinds of outrageous thinking and do all kinds of absurd things. We often wonder where they came from until we get to know them, and then we conclude that they are no more outrageous or absurd than we are. But managers have no alternative but to find a way to deal with these differences and idiosyncrasies. Getting to know something about the people that you work with poses a major challenge.

As a professional you have probably worked with managers who functioned at different points on the continuum, ranging from aggressive and proactive at one end to reactive and inactive at the other end. Other managers displayed different characteristics depending on the nature of the work at the time: aggressive and proactive at one time and reactive and inactive at another time. Being aggressive and proactive should not be construed to mean making impossible demands or being disrespectful or rude or insolent. Aggressive and proactive applies to the attitude toward accomplishing goals and objectives; it implies not just being on the leading edge but taking the lead. Goals and objectives are reached through discipline. Why can one orchestra conductor obtain superior performance from an orchestra while another conducting the same musicians only receives a mediocre response? The aggressive and proactive people will be looked upon as the high-performance benchmarks. Reactive and inactive managers are generally crisis driven; every day brings on a new set of crises because future events are not anticipated. These managers tend to play the role of the storekeeper rather than the store owner. So from your past experience you know managers are just as complex as their employees and come in just as many varieties. What kind of a manager do you want to be?

Successful teams demonstrate a sense of enthusiasm and a sense of excitement. This becomes evident the minute you walk into a department. Putting everybody in his or her own cubicle has made this more difficult, but can be demonstrated when you are in contact with working groups. The sense of interest, mutual cooperation, consideration for other's requirements, and total involvement becomes evident very quickly. There's a give and take on issues. Arguments and dissent are resolved through dialogue. Note that there's a distinction between discussion and dialogue. Discussion usually involves talking around issues and voicing opinions without focusing on the real issues and reaching conclusions. Dialogue involves free access and sharing of information, challenging of assumptions, bringing conflicts to the surface and resolving them to the satisfaction of all concerned, giving due consideration to alternatives, and in the process building intellectual trust.

Members of a successful team develop a high level of trust. They are stimulated by their work and that stimulation rubs off on every member. There is no fear of judgment on raising issues because the focus is on performance. Did you ever work in what I refer to as a *blah* organization or department: an organization or department that exuded apathy and aloofness about meeting goals and objectives and the need for adding value through their work effort? What a waste of talent and other resources. Intellectual and operational discipline just doesn't exist. There's not much incentive to come to work under such conditions.

BUILDING THE TEAM

Teams are not a management panacea; they are useful in certain situations and not in others. They enhance or hinder an operation depending on the team members and the purposes for which the team has been established. Managers need to be cautious about adopting team concepts without adequate knowledge. Teams can work only after a major investment in education of the total organization. I stress education here rather than training, and education for the whole organization rather than some few senior project managers.

If people are to be able to move from team to team they must understand the basics of team operations and practice to allow them to make the cultural shifts as they move from one department or project to another. Following some predetermined process won't work because it doesn't take the people requirements into account. There is no handbook approach that paves the way. We need to be cautious in how we manage teams to counter William H. Whyte's argument that group activity (teams) has a downward leveling effect on the individual, forces conformity, denies expression of individualism, nullifies creative activity, and in general hampers and limits human activity.

Teamwork is no longer an option. But teamwork involves more than selecting a group of bodies to meet some goal or objective. The key to successful team performance involves integrating the minds, competencies, skills, and attitudes of the team members to focus on the goals and objectives for which the team was organized. It also includes providing education and training, but it's too late to provide the education and training only when the team is formed.

Most activities that require the *act of doing* cannot be taught from a book. Yes, the basics and some ground rules can be learned, but they're only the starting point for implementation. There are many formal courses sponsored through consultants, industrial training organizations, and academic institutions. I propose that team building must be accomplished within the particular context in which it will occur. Team building at McDonald's will be quite different from team building at General Electric. Team building at Boeing will be quite different from team building at Microsoft. While the fundamentals are the same, the context and scope are totally different and thus require a different approach.

Team building cannot be considered as an isolated event independent of other organizational requirements. Team-building exercises need to be integrated into the issues currently faced by the organization. It is not enough to send the team leader to a workshop on team building. The complete team must understand the fundamental issues that drive team performance. We know from experience that most teams include a few full-time members and many other participants whose services do not justify full-time participation. People may also serve on more than one team. So the department manager must educate all department members about personal expectations and team functions. The greatest benefits arise when team-building education is performed within the context of the department's activities. You're dealing in the real world.

So, how do you find time to build team competence when you're already supposedly overworked? Teams generally meet to discuss results as well as upcoming concerns. Reserve just one hour per week and begin teaching team concepts in relation to the work at hand. Once the process begins, team members will become more enthusiastic because much of the blaming will be eliminated. Whether your team benefits from learning depends on their confidence in speaking what's on their mind, their ability to admit mistakes and learn from them, and on whether they have access to the required intellectual property of the organization, use their ability to question intelligently, and have freedom to challenge management. Learning requires this kind of openness. Members of the team cannot hold back their concerns; they must be brought out for critical analysis and disposition.

In an environment in which freedom to raise controversial issues exists without threatening the messenger, you can begin by teaching the fundamentals like framing the problem, developing the objectives, evaluating critical issues, reaching agreement and making decisions, communicating information, and also discussing how human behavior affects all these processes. But this teaching and learning takes place in the context of the work at hand. You're teaching and learning through solving real problems, not some abstract problems. You are solving those problems with your people and not with some idealized grouping of team members.

LEARNING FROM RESEARCH

True or false: teams that follow a structured process provide better solutions. Consider the results of research carried out by John C. Redding, whose research includes studies of two sets of teams.[2]

Team A was involved in a high-profile initiative in which the team was asked to accelerate the schedule requested by a customer. The team meeting took place in elegant surroundings with highly skilled middle managers from leading graduate business schools, and with a well-developed agenda. The team was challenged to make quick decisions and use systematic risk analysis. The team meeting was well planned and executed. The team decided to decline to accelerate the schedule requested by customer.

Team B was formed to recommend whether the company should introduce a low-cost, off-the-shelf product line. The team includes production supervisors and machine operators from manufacturing, only a few had college degrees, and no formal team training. The meeting was held in a crammed lunchroom with no formal agenda and no plan. The team was entrenched in two camps, emotions were high, people interrupted each other in mid-sentence, and name-calling was frequent. One of the vocal advocates for a particular position became very angry and left the room with a threat to quit the organization. The group was stunned. In an attempt to deal with the situation the team started talking about starting a company from scratch for this low-end market. They explored ways to streamline production and identified ways to standardize the product line. The discussion became more and more serious as the discussion continued. There was excitement. They discussed the possibilities of a stand-alone company. They met again two weeks later, and within six months the *new company* was launched.

What happened here? Team A was a highly skilled group of managers who lived up to the status quo; no exploration of alternative and no innovation. Team B, although undisciplined and at times unruly, transformed the company. Redding raises the question: Did the messiness of Team B with its frequent impasses and tension stimulate an innovative business solution and a commitment to make it happen?

Redding's questions were answered and were reinforced from research by Laurel Jeris[3] in 1997. Jeris formed eighty, five-person teams, and divided them into two sets. One set was structured as Team A and the other set, without any guidance or help, was similar to Team B. The results: teams trained to follow prescribed teamwork practices (like Team A) were less apt to create innovative solutions if left to their own devices. The teams left on their own (like Team B) were twice as likely to develop innovative solutions. Jeris then set up a third group of teams with a set of guidelines that asked them to separate facts from assumptions and not blindly accept the problem as presented. These teams rephrased their problems three times as often as those using traditional team problem-solving methods. The results suggest the possibility of a new model for teamwork designed to increase the reexamination of how problems are framed.

What conclusions can we draw from this research? Team A went through the process with competent people that accepted the problem as it was given. There were no dissident voices. There really was no dialogue. No one raised doubts about the problem statement. This was a typical session by knowledgeable though not necessarily competent or proactive managers. The tough questions were not asked. Team B was a freewheeling team meeting that to the casual observer would seem chaotic. There was no defined process for reaching a conclusion. Do we thus conclude that a process is not required? No. Following a process wasn't what prevented Team A from finding a way of meeting the customer's request. The problem was the manner in which they approached the problem. The session really didn't consider alternatives to resolving the problem. No creativity. No innovation. Do it the same way as we always have done it.

Do we then conclude that the chaotic approach used by Team B is the right way? Probably not. It will take time to repair the destructive effects on personal relationships. But Team B came up with an innovative solution in spite of its chaotic meeting. I suggest that process is important but the process must make allowances for reaching the appropriate solution. Every process involves going through a series of steps to reach some conclusion. But it also includes going through that process considering alternatives. It involves validating the definition of the problem and developing the evidence to confirm that the real problem is under consideration. The problem must be framed. Framing is defined by Schön[4] as:

> The process by which we define the decision to be made, the
> ends to be achieved, the means which may be chosen. In real-

world practice, problems do not present themselves to the practitioner as givens. They must be constructed from materials of problematic situations which are puzzling, troubling, and uncertain. In order to convert a problematic situation to a problem a practitioner must do a certain kind of work. He must make sense of an uncertain situation that initially makes no sense.

Jeris's third group, who reframed their problem many times, provides a better model than either Team A or Team B followed.

ASKING THE QUESTIONS AND GETTING THE ANSWERS

From research on teams and my own personal experiences over many years in managing team activities I suggest that the following issues require specific responses if a team hopes to meet its objectives.

1. Define the problem or opportunity under consideration. Keep in mind that open dialogue may require redrafting the problem statement many times.

2. Frame the problem. What are we doing? Why are we doing this? How are we going to do it? Who is responsible for doing it? When do we do it? Where do we do it? What are the expected outcomes?

3. Describe the specific mix of competencies required to solve the problem or pursue some new opportunity. Are they available either within or outside the department or the organization? If not, how do you resolve the issue?

4. Develop open communication. How does the team communicate? From where does it take its cues in reaching decisions? Does the team allow the difficult questions to surface?

5. Propose a defined communication structure and network that defines what should be communicated, when, and

by whom and to whom. There's no room for comments like "Why didn't you tell me?"

6. Define the roles and responsibilities clearly, anticipate the gaps, and integrate them in relation to the requirements.

7. Problem-solving skills do not necessarily come naturally. They must be grounded in some methodology. Whatever process is used it must be consistent and the team must be aware of the protocols.

8. Problem-finding skills are equally important to problem-solving skills. Every defined problem has within it some unfound problems that need a resolution.

9. All team members require some knowledge in making timely decisions. They need to understand decision processes and their role in reaching decisions.

10. Team reviews cannot become typical dog-and-pony shows that exclude a dialogue about current or potential difficulties in meeting the objectives. Reviews are learning experiences that ask the difficult questions.

11. Conflict can have a positive or negative impact. It's positive if it raises the issues that some may not wish to raise. It's negative when it becomes personal and disregards the facts.

12. Playing catch-up to competitors doesn't inspire a team. Creativity allows the team to take the lead and to work on the leading edge. If you're in the game, why not play to win?

13. Innovation allows the team to break away from the pack. Innovation is more than creativity; it's a focus on invention and implementation.

These thirteen competencies and skills determine whether the team will meet its objectives. Competent teams function in an entrepreneurial mode in which all the team members are owners; they own the project and treat it accordingly.

DEFINING THE ROLE OF THE INDIVIDUAL

Defining the role of any person requires knowledge about that person. But that knowledge includes more than knowing about the person's specialized competency, credentials, and peer comments. Some brilliant people too often fail to live up to their brilliance. They may be well learned and be storehouses of information but lack the ability to translate information into action. They often fail to demonstrate the drive and dedication needed to meet their goals. Some people are very vocal but not necessarily articulate, and they gain attention that is somehow translated into competence. The people who appear to be not involved may be the best contributors. They work diligently in their own quiet way, not seeking attention. Certain people ask many questions but seldom provide any answers. People who may not display any particular brilliance in any facet of their work sometimes have the capability to somehow put it all together. These are the people who integrate their knowledge, skills, competencies, and attitudes into a workable package.

Assignments should be made based on needs. As a manager you must decide what knowledge, skills, attitudes, personal characteristics, and experience are required to fulfill the job requirements. But don't expect to meet those requirements at one hundred percent. Not even you would meet them. Competent managers maintain a profile on their people and update those profiles as new information is generated. As noted previously disregard the credentials and focus on the past accomplishments and the track record. Through these profiles you can determine what new experiences should be provided and what new educational opportunities may be required for future growth. These profiles are the manager's working documents and are not meant for storage in the human resource archives.

Too often we tend to place people in boxes and don't let them get out. As a manager you need knowledgeable professionals who are low-key and unassuming as well as those who are driven and energetic. You need the theorists and the practitioners. You'd also like to have people who link theory and practice. You also need people who are willing to try doing something even though they know nothing about what they're doing; these people need your guidance and direction. You need people who will do the grunt work. You need people, often referred to as the plodders, who do just what they're asked to do.

So as you structure teams, whether large or small, simple or complex, or short or long term, you need to determine competencies required to meet the objectives. There are no simple answers; just determine what your people are capable of doing. Don't assign a competent person with a phlegmatic personality to a position that requires a driven and energetic personality. Don't assign a person who excels at research-type activities to a routine although important position. Don't assign responsibilities to those not meeting the requirements and hope for the best. You must provide guidance and education to give your staff the opportunity to succeed.

USING TEAMS EFFECTIVELY

Peter Senge,[5] author of *The Fifth Discipline,* asks the question, "How can a team of committed managers with individual IQs of 120 have a collective IQ of 63?" Chris Argyris[5] writes in *The Fifth Discipline* that most management teams break down under pressure. The team may function quite well with routine issues. But when they confront complex issues that may be embarrassing or threatening, the *teamness* seems to go to pot.

Senge was referring primarily to upper management teams. But we find the similar conditions for teams made up primarily of professional specialists. Collective inquiry can be threatening because individual preferences and actions must be justified and this forces examination of traditional approaches and methodologies. Professionals are just as resistant to change as the general population. Someone's favorite process, or technology, or planning system, or component, or material has been working for years, so why change it? It's easier to go with the old rather than take the risk with the new, the unknown. It's easier to tweak the system than to explore new opportunities.

Collective inquiry forces us to find new ways to solve problems that will accommodate the needs of other professional specialists. It forces us to give up the old for the new but with some logical justification. It forces new thinking to determine whether our demands really exist, and find out if our position involves certain biases or just our inability to face the uncertainties and risks. It forces us to examine whether or not the tried and true methods continue to provide a benefit in a dynamic and interconnected society. Argyris refers to this position of refusing to face up to reality as *skilled incompetence,* teams made up of exceedingly capable people who keep themselves from learning.

There is no doubt that problems are more complex today than in the past. Finding solutions requires input from many disciplines. Managing those professional interfaces takes not only knowledge and skills but also determination on the part of all the participants to reach an equitable and viable solution. That solution will involve compromises, but those compromises cannot go against the basic tenets of any discipline involved.

Team participants do not have to love each other. They do have to show respect and common courtesy as they would to any person. They may or may not socialize; there should be no required attendance at the Friday after-work session to get to know each other. They do have to communicate and listen to each other. They must consider the views and needs of others. They must bury their egos. They can't fight turf wars. They must face reality and deal with their problems. They must focus on delivering the outcomes of the project that they were assigned.

These conditions are common to all teams regardless of discipline. The process is so simple; define the purposes and objectives of the project; select the team based on the required competencies; develop the plan and the criteria for measuring performance; communicate, communicate, and communicate some more; resolve the interface problems; begin the dialogue; lay all the cards on the table, face up; identify the different points of view and search for common ground; don't be afraid of creating some cognitive dissonance to bring problems to the surface early in the project—but difficult to implement.

PURSUING EXCELLENCE

How do managers pursue excellence in team performance? Excellence is in the eyes of the beholder. However, the meaning of the word *excellence* has been significantly diminished in recent times. Much of today's *excellence* is equivalent to yesterday's *mediocrity.* Instead of raising performance standards because of the management tools available, we continue to lower them by making allowances for and justifying nonperformance. These lower standards are demonstrated in every profession and in every line of work.

Managers also need to bring the right tools to the job; those tools include the ability to think and think deeply before making serious decisions. Pursuing excellence is hard work; it involves total dedication toward some objective.

Managers have the responsibility for setting the pace, for setting the performance standards, and for raising the expectations of the team. Setting the pace involves establishing stretch targets that force the team to examine its work methods and find the ones that are most appropriate. Following the same process because it's known and easy isn't acceptable. Setting performance standards at all professional levels involves considering the alternatives and then selecting the best solution that meets the requirements. If a cookie-cutter approach meets the requirements, use it, but make sure you're using the right cookie cutter. Raising expectations from the team involves reducing time and cost, improving quality of work methods and work output, eliminating communication barriers, and enforcing discipline. Discipline as used here means mental discipline, mastering the body of knowledge and theory and technique for effective application.

Not all team members will live up to expectations regardless of the approach and energy dedicated to selecting the team. There will be obstructionists because their talent may be essential. There will also be the socializing loafers. It may be necessary to put up with the obstructionists if the competence or skills they bring to the table are absolutely essential. I define an obstructionist as one who always challenges everyone and everything regardless of the issue but seldom offers any constructive alternative. Don't equate the obstructionist with the constructive maverick who raises questions others failed to ask, but also works toward a resolution of those differences. The obstructionist must be controlled; the constructive maverick should be encouraged. Socializing loafers also need to be controlled because they waste time for others; they also become the rumor messengers. Most loafing takes place when people do not have enough work to keep them fully occupied. The problem can be curtailed and eliminated by increasing the workload.

MAKING DIVERSITY WORK

Why should you as an entry-level manager concern yourself about diversity? There's a simple answer—federal and state laws that govern discrimination. But as a manager the expectations include more than just fulfilling legal requirements. Your management will expect you to meet the legal requirements and at the same time appoint the best-qualified people to achieve your unit's goals and objectives. But finding and selecting the best-qualified people involves not only the best in a particular professional discipline but those with the required breadth of knowledge, an attitude toward meeting commitments, the essential personal characteristics like integrity and dedication, the skills like leadership and communication, and the ability to work effectively with people who come to the workplace from different cultures. You'll be expected to blend these people who may have significantly different social, political, and economic orientations into a cohesive organizational unit—people who view the organization and the environment differently and who bring very different backgrounds and perspectives to the workplace.

The Diversity Challenge

Diversity is not a human resources problem but an organizational opportunity—an opportunity to maximize the performance of an organization. Since you come to this position after some years of experience as a competent professional you have already witnessed what your organization and others have done or not done to promote diversity. Workplace diversity presents a challenge to all managers.

A description of what diversity involves provides a better approach to discussing the related issues than providing a definition. Diversity involves dealing with differences and finding a way to resolve those differences in some acceptable manner. The primary diversity issue is avoiding discrimination because of race, culture, gender, sexual orientation, age, religious beliefs, and physical disabilities, hereafter referred to as the *basic diversity group*. Resolving the issues related to the constituents of this group becomes complicated because we bring our prejudices, our opinions, those often intolerable habits, and all the baggage that makes us, us.

We also bring all of the experiences that brought us to our present state of being—cultures in which we lived, successes and failures experienced, relationships developed, influences on our thinking by those many teachers both formal and informal, and just about every act that in some way influenced our being. Only by finding a way to accommodate all of these differences can we develop viable organizations that meet their purposes and objectives. At the same time we need to recognize that utopia does not exist. This is not a perfect world. People often pursue particular agendas that can have a significant negative impact on overall performance. That's the real world. So as a new manager, how do you respond to these diversity issues?

Diversity Initiatives

David A. Thomas and Robin J. Ely[6] suggest that two perspectives have guided most diversity initiatives: (1) equal opportunity, fair treatment, recruitment, and compliance with federal and state laws and regulations, and (2) it just makes good business sense. A third perspective focuses on diversity because it's the right thing to do. Do we really need government regulations to provide equal opportunity and fair treatment? The human condition being what it is suggests that government regulations are essential. As a manager you have no alternative but to be knowledgeable about the rules and regulations related to fair treatment of all individuals regardless of their orientation. Lack of concern about fairness could not only have a negative financial impact on the organization but also cause a significant loss in reputation.

In cold hard numbers promoting diversity makes good sense. This has nothing to do with the organization's moral or social orientation—it serves the interest of the organization and the community. It's enlightened self-interest. But diversity is not about numbers and quotas: it's about enabling the required talent to freely participate in an organization's future. Talent is in limited supply. We live in a global economy in which national cultures come together to fulfill some purpose. There was a time when all the talent and wisdom resided in the motherhouse. That is no longer true. As organizations expanded globally (this was not just a U.S. phenomenon) they recognized the talent and wisdom available in other nations. They recognized that cultural differences had to be accommodated and integrated in order to meet transnational goals and objectives. This expansion phenomenon also includes academic institutions that have expanded into other countries.

There's nothing magic about dealing with diversity. There are no pre-
scriptions because every breach of diversity presents unique issues. Like
any management issue it requires understanding and using some very com-
mon-sense approaches. People wish to be treated fairly and with respect
regardless of the differences that might separate them from the group in
some way. The issue of fairness is open to interpretation and cannot be
measured on some mathematical scale. You may think that the action you
have taken was fair but an employee may think your decision was unfair.
Such conflicts can only be resolved through communication that deals
solely with the facts. Those facts are open to interpretation. Each is probably looking at the issue from a different perspective. You or the employee
could be either right or wrong in reaching conclusions. As the manager
you must take responsibility for resolving the issue quickly. An unresolved
issue only leads to a lack of commitment, little if any contribution to
productivity, and a negative impact on the other members of your group.

Accommodating Differences

Let's face the facts: we're all different, we may hold minor prejudices, and
we probably judge others by higher standards than we use to judge ourselves. Demographic statistics show that our workplaces now include
many people from the basic diversity group of constituents. Workplaces
are no longer a collection of homogeneous people where one size fits all.
Any application of a one-size-fits-all philosophy will only lead to major
behavioral problems. So you learn how to accommodate differences. At
the same time you cannot capitulate on every issue that is vital for maintaining some level of management discipline. Some rules are required. You
can't allow one person to disrupt the whole organization. But you do establish limits in which the organization can function effectively and efficiently.

You also need to be more sensitive to individual styles and behaviors.
Being sensitive to behaviors does not imply lowering performance requirements or accepting lower levels of performance. It does not imply being
overzealously sympathetic or promoting a victim mentality but it does
imply responsiveness, reassurance, and empathy. You and your colleagues
will engage people whose personal working habits and customs may be

objectionable in some way. You may in some way temper their impact but you will not eliminate them. To avoid any signs of discrimination, base your decisions on the individual's contributions and not the personal likes or dislikes of their habits or customs. There is no justification for discriminating against any individual because he or she is a member of the basic diversity group.

Relieving Tension

A certain amount of tension always exists when people from different origins meet. People who in some way do not meet our perceptions can be suspect. They're different. That tension can either be creative or destructive. As we begin to know a person tensions begin to disappear. We accept them, perhaps not totally, but we accept them for what they are. We accept them for their knowledge or skill or accomplishments. At a minimum we show respect. We relieve those tensions by learning about them. We recognize their presence and communicate with them. We try to find some common ground. There may be a common interest; a similar academic background; common family activities; related work experiences; knowledge of each other's national histories; interests in sports, the arts, volunteer activities; and other interests too numerous to mention. When we find these common areas of interest we begin building a new relationship. But we need to find those areas of common interest to relieve the tension. So while we may be initially concerned about certain origins, personal attitudes and characteristics, and behavioral patterns we accept people because of some common interests. When the tension disappears we accept people for what they are rather than what we think they should be. The stereotypes tend to disappear.

3M is a company that has always valued diversity in its workforce. It could not have accomplished its status as a global innovator without embracing the broad requirements for managing diversity. The following is an interesting 3M story of how inappropriate dress colored the perception of competence by some laboratory directors:

> Many years ago the standard of dress for executives, managers, and professionals was the typical business suit and tie. Researchers also came to work in business suits or some less

formal wear. In the mid- to late sixties some researchers began coming to work in sport shirts, sweat shirts, ponytails, beards, and sandals. Many research directors didn't know how to deal with such situations. These weird forms of dress and behavior were upsetting the status quo. These newcomers didn't fit the mold.

In the final analysis reason prevailed. At a meeting of the organization's laboratory directors the vice president of research asked a very simple question; are you hiring the ponytails and sandals or are you hiring the innovation competence that these people bring to your laboratory? The logical response favored innovation competence but some doubters persisted. These newcomers were highly competent people but chose to change the research culture as it related to dress standards. One of these researchers eventually became one of the company's top inventors. He was respected for his accomplishments and people learned to disregard his style of dress. Eventually the dress fad went the way of all fads and was replaced by more moderate dress.

Some Guidelines

You should accept managing diversity issues as just one more management responsibility. The issues involve your staff and you as a manager. These issues may or may not arise but be prepared to deal with them with the help of the human resources department and/or the legal department. Problems often begin with an offhand remark by one of your staff to another member that may have been misinterpreted. That same remark could have been intentional. There may be some act against a staff member from any of the basic diversity group constituents. As a manager you need to resolve these issues immediately. They cannot be allowed to fester and grow in intensity. The extent to which diversity issues require involvement of the human resource and legal departments depend on your ability to identify potential problems in their early stages, determine the causes, resolve them immediately if possible, and provide any additional diversity training that may be required. You also set the tone for your organizational unit through your own actions.

Dealing with the *basic diversity group* issues can be managed more easily by developing a culture of collegiality, establishing working policies and practices that maximize the use of available talent, and providing opportunities for individual growth by developing people to be the best that they can be independent of any alignment with the basic diversity group constituents. A culture of colleagues excludes no one who meets the basic skills and competencies to do the work regardless of position or level. The manager's responsibility is to select the best-qualified person, keeping in mind that job requirements vary over a very broad spectrum in every discipline. Alignment with any of the constituents of the basic diversity group should not enter the decision except if a particular orientation is required.

The organization's policies and practices must support collegiality. Actions that ignore those policies only work against developing an inclusive culture that fosters diversity. How managers choose people for developing new competencies that provide them with opportunities for growth and advancement demonstrates the importance of using diversity as a means for maximizing an organization's use of resources. Diversity is more than just tolerating those individual differences that may make us uncomfortable.

We need to be cautious in evaluating people according to our personal prejudices and stereotypes. Prejudice for or against a certain employee will be met with concern. Prejudice for may not allow the employee to fulfill expectations because of lack of ability. Prejudice against may not only destroy trust but eventually cause the loss of a competent employee.

The model for developing a department that fosters diversity and maximizes not only the competencies of the group but also provides for developing new competencies is relatively simple.

❑ Accept the differences in people and build upon them.

❑ Promote free expression and dialogue.

❑ Set high standards.

❑ Value your workers.

❑ Focus on the unit's mission.

❑ Show respect for people and their idiosyncrasies.

❑ Create a community that shares its values.

❑ Promote differences but seek agreement.

❑ Diffuse any animosities through education.

❑ Encourage communication.

❑ Don't talk down to anybody.

❑ Encourage and critique intelligently.

MOTIVATING THE TEAM

Managers influence and motivate their people and their organizations. The question is, how? We need not concern ourselves about the small percentage of people who are self-motivated. These people somehow find something positive in every action even though it leads to temporary detours or failures. They have no difficulty recovering from those supposed failures that often open new avenues for exploration.

There are two types of motivation: intrinsic and extrinsic. People who are intrinsically motivated receive satisfaction from developing their own capabilities through self-discovery and self-development. Personal growth dominates their actions. They have an ever-present desire for originating or participating in new experiences. Rewards for performance are not a major issue. Extrinsic motivation includes all the tangibles like compensation, advancement, fringe benefits, challenging work assignments, special perks, and any other symbols or actions that differentiated the contributions of individual workers.

There are no "yes" or "no" answers to motivating a group. Well-motivated team members have a certain something that attracts others. They have an ability to set the mood. They're not the *rah rah* people, but are simply people who have the ability to bring others along. Managers need to recognize that motivating the group involves taking advantage of all the talent available. People respond differently based on their personal needs for job satisfaction. Abraham Maslow, Frederick Herzberg, and Douglas McGregor set forth some guiding principles that you need to consider.

Maslow[7] presented a hierarchy of needs that states that the lower level needs must be provided before the higher level needs become important. Maslow's hierarchy of needs involves meeting:

❑ **Physiological needs, which include basic life-sustaining elements like food, water, air, environmental, and so on.**

❑ Safety needs, which include feelings of security, being free from danger and threats, good health, and stability.

❑ Social needs, which include acceptance by others, respect from others, a sense of belonging, and community affiliation.

❑ Self-esteem needs, which are fulfilled by recognition and respect from colleagues and by voiced approval from others.

❑ Self-actualization needs, which relate to finding self-fulfillment opportunities on which to build a career.

Maslow's hierarchy of needs provides a general guideline of how personal needs are met but as always there are inconsistencies. The driven person often achieves major breakthroughs even when the basic requirements of survival such as food are not available. The higher level needs may be totally disregarded because of a particular drive to accomplish some objective. The list ranges from people like Madame Curie, the discoverer of radium, who lived on radishes and worked in an intolerable environment, to today's entrepreneurs, who sacrifice comfort and security and mortgage all their assets and often come close to mortgaging their families to realize their goals. However, it is important that you be aware of Maslow's hierarchy of needs. You're really looking for people whose self-esteem needs are fulfilled through accomplishments and not some self-esteem building program. You're looking for self-actualized people who find self-fulfillment opportunities on which to build a career. It's difficult to build a team with people who focus only on their physiological, safety, and social needs.

Frederick Herzberg's[8] research considered the differences between what he referred to as hygiene factors and motivation. He found that peoples' attitudes toward aspects of their jobs that are generally considered motivators basically contributed to job satisfaction and not motivation. He referred to these as *hygiene factors*, which included company policies, supervision, interpersonal relations, working conditions, and salary and benefits. Their absence caused dissatisfaction but their presence did not increase motivation. Herzberg's motivators included achievement, recognition, work itself, responsibility, and advancement.

It's difficult to argue with Herzberg's conclusions. From years of experience and contact with hundreds of managers, I've found that motivation depends on the people within a team who have the energy and enthusiasm to move the team to greater accomplishment because the work is challenging. Yes, they want the recognition and added responsibility, but the means toward achieving that end involves challenging work. Herzberg's motivation may be summarized as follows: forget praise, forget punishment, forget cash; make their jobs more interesting instead.

In 1956, the Alfred P. Sloan Foundation made a grant to Douglas McGregor[9] and Alex Bavelas to explore the issue of whether successful managers were born or made. This effort was an attempt to substantiate the thesis that the human side of enterprise is about how management perceives its role of controlling the human resources that determine the character of the organization. The authors decided that the key question for managers is: "What are the key assumptions (implicit as well as explicit) about the best way to manage people?"

This research effort yielded the concepts of the Theory X and Theory Y managers. Theory X managers assume that the average human being has an inherent dislike for work and will avoid it if possible, and that most people must be coerced, controlled, directed, and threatened to put forth adequate effort. Average human beings prefer to be directed, wish to avoid responsibility, have relatively little ambition, and want security above all other benefits. You have probably met some of these people in your professional work life and possibly among your social contacts. There is a body of evidence to support Theory X. Theory X as a managerial strategy doesn't work with professionals as a rule, but I have seen these principles applied successfully with several super-competent scientific researchers. It does appear that some very highly skilled professionals need to be controlled because they lack ambition and often do not know just how to get started. They often fail to know how to work and become involved in pursuing non-essential details.

Theory Y, as you may surmise, is at the other end of this control-and-freedom continuum. Theory Y is based on the principles that:

1. The expenditure of physical and mental effort in work is as natural as play and rest. [Comment: *It's not* quite *the same as play and rest.*]

2. External control and threat of punishment are not the only means of bringing about effort toward organizational objectives. [Comment: *Agree, but punishment may be necessary and productive at times, if applied judiciously.*]

3. Commitment to objectives depends on the rewards associated with achievement. [Comment: *Yes and no; commitment is often given freely without any rewards.*]

4. The average human being learns not only to accept but to seek responsibility. [Comment: *It's all about accepting personal responsibility for one's future.*]

5. The possibility to exercise a relatively high degree of imagination, ingenuity, and creativity in the solution of organizational problems is widely distributed in the population. [Comment: *Employees may possess these competencies, but they need the will and determination to pursue them to a conclusion.*]

6. Under conditions of modern industrial life, the intellectual capabilities of the average human being are significantly underutilized. [Comment: *This represents a significant loss to organizations and to their people—people underutilization is a career death sentence.*]

Theory X and Y have never really been proven but we can rationalize them with some degree of logic. Theory X is based on direction and control; Theory Y is based on integration where members of the organization can achieve their own goals by directing their efforts toward the success of the organization. The question usually asked–*Are you a Theory X or Theory Y manager?*–doesn't make any sense. While many managers fall at the extreme ends of this continuum, competent managers fall someplace on that continuum and exhibit the characteristics of X and Y depending on the situation.

Motivation begins by recognizing that people have different needs. The increased diversity of the workforce has brought the issue of individual differences into sharper focus. We know that providing for individual differences determines performance. However, managers cannot agree to provide for all those individual differences. The organization does not exist solely to fulfill personal needs. It does have a self-interest in meeting those needs to the extent possible, but not by taking away personal responsibility. As a manager you decide just how far you'll go to accommodate those differences. You motivate by challenging all members to exceed performance targets by clearing away obstacles and taking part in the action. Don't micromanage, but get involved.

PROMOTING SELF-MANAGED TEAMS

Although much has been written about self-managed teams, it's difficult to find positive results. The idea that five or ten or twenty people could accomplish anything without some person taking the responsibility for the results appears to go against all management theory and practice. Just think about two people interacting and reaching a conclusion. The fact remains that at some point in time someone must make the decision. A lifetime cannot be spent attempting to reach consensus. Not even a family has the luxury of functioning without someone taking responsibility. Someone must eventually decide where they're going, when, and for what reason. Chances of meeting expectations in a self-managed team are not very good.

But here is one example of a self-managed team. The Orpheus Chamber Orchestra, established for more than thirty years, is recognized as one of the world's major symphonic organizations.[10] It rehearses and performs without a director. It has developed a self-governing structure that emphasizes collaborative leadership. Orchestra participants resolve their differences by building on three team-building principles: preparation, communication, and mutual respect. They admit it takes a great deal of time to resolve issues.

This multiple nondesignated leader concept may be applied to all organizations with the major drawback being the length of time it takes to resolve differences. We also need to recognize that the orchestra is a very special type of organization; the participants are all high-level professionals in their chosen vocation and play from the same sheet of music. While it may work with a limited number of people, I question the results if applied to an organization of several hundred people.

SUMMARY

- ❏ A team is a group of people that develops a collective state of mind. It's a thinking organism where problems are defined, assumptions challenged, solutions provided, and results assessed.

- ❏ Team building is a continuous process and not a single event. It takes place within the daily activities of the department. It involves solving real problems facing the department.

- ❏ As the team leader you set the direction and the style. You establish the required discipline. You set the standards. You determine whether your department finishes first, last, or somewhere in between.

- ❏ Research tells us that following specific processes without considering alternatives may not lead to the most appropriate solution. Who sits at the decision table is not important; who *thinks* at the decision table is important.

- ❏ Teams only achieve lasting success by paying attention to the details. Those difficult questions must be answered. The competencies must be available when needed.

- ❏ The role of each team member must be defined. You as the team leader decide which competencies, skills, attitudes, and characteristics are required. Job descriptions aren't necessary.

- ❏ Effective use of teams involves complex interactions among many disciplines. Collective inquiry allows us to find new ways of solving problems in order to meet the needs of all related disciplines.

- ❏ There is no alternative to pursuing excellence. Anything less only produces obsolescence and the associated problems.

- ❏ Diversity involves more than just avoiding discrimination of the constituents of the basic diversity group. The new paradigm promotes opportunities for all individuals and acknowledges cultural differences and recognizes the value of those differences.

❑ Motivation determines whether or not the department produces the desired outcomes. Bells and whistles aren't required; just provide challenging work that allows the team to
become involved.

❑ If you want to try a self-managed team, be my guest. It's a
nice concept to dream about but in today's world we still have
to *pin the rose* on some one.

NOTES

1. Allan Cox, "The Homework Behind Teamwork," *Industry Week*, January 7, 1991.
2. John C. Redding, *The Radical Team Handbook* (San Francisco: Jossey-
   Bass, 2000), pp. 5–12.
3. L. Jeris, "An Empirical Study of the Relationship Between Team Process Interventions and Double-Loop Learning." Unpublished doctoral
   dissertation, Department of Leadership and Educational Policy Studies, Northern Illinois University, 1997.
4. D. Schön, *The Reflective Practitioner: How Professionals Think in Action*
   (New York: Basic Books, 1983), p. 40.
5. Peter M. Senge, *The Fifth Discipline* (New York: Doubleday Currency,
   1990), pp. 3–25.
6. David A.S. Thomas and Robin J. Ely, "Making Differences Matter:
   A New Paradigm for Managing Diversity," *Harvard Business Review*,
   September–October 1996, pp. 79–90.
7. Abraham H. Maslow, *Motivation and Personality* (New York: Harper &
   Row, 1970).
8. Frederick Herzberg, "One More Time: How Do You Motivate Employees?" *Harvard Business Review*, 1986. Reprint No. 388X, January
   2003.
9. Douglas McGregor, *The Human Side of Enterprise* (New York: Mc-
   Graw-Hill, 1960), pp. 3–57.
10. Chris Maxwell, "Conductor-Less Yet Leader-Full: What Business Can
    Learn from the Orpheus Chamber Orchestra," *Wharton Leadership
    Digest* 7, 2 (2002).

CHAPTER 5

Project Management

This chapter applies the principles of managing individual and team relationships to the project management process. In recent years project management (PM) has gained recognition as a way of managing organizational activities. At one time the use of PM was restricted primarily to the research, development, and manufacturing functions, but now organizations have expanded its application to all functions.

Unfortunately, sometimes too much emphasis is placed on PM tools. Tools are important, but they are not the major priority in implementing the PM process. The difficulty lies in selecting the right tools and then applying them effectively to meet the requirements. Many PM tools include too much data, which provides little if any benefit for the effort expended. The benefit of PM lies in going through the thought processes (the real work) required to frame the project and determine its viability in a particular organizational context.

As a newly appointed manager your responsibility also includes developing competent project managers who meet project specifications, complete projects on time, and do not exceed cost projections for all projects in your department and for those in which you partner with other departments. These projects will vary in size, scope, complexity, and any number of other variables depending on your department's and the organization's purposes. We'll consider the issues that seldom receive sufficient attention, which are:

- ❏ Project design
- ❏ Types of projects
- ❏ Evaluating proposed projects
- ❏ The project process
- ❏ Multidisciplinary and multifunctional projects
- ❏ Managing projects across cultures
- ❏ Strategic project management

PROJECT DESIGN

Project design plays a major role in meeting project expectations. (Note: The word *design* has a broad meaning in this context. It is not restricted to technology-related activities or the arts. Projects are designed with specific purposes. The project design involves considering all of the elements required to produce a positive outcome.) The project design focuses primarily on the thinking required to define a project and bring it to a successful conclusion. We know from research that less than ten percent of projects fulfill their specifications, within the estimated timeline, and at the estimated costs. The statistics on information systems projects are even worse. As a newly appointed manager you probably come with some knowledge of project management, but you need to understand why so few projects meet all requirements. Many of the reasons for not meeting project outcomes, such as change in scope, lack of resources, loss of a key employee, and a week of snowstorms, are simply not acceptable.

As the newly appointed manager, you should review the past history of the department you have inherited and see what percentage of projects met the required outcomes during the past year, and determine the reasons they did or did not. What you learn from this past history, coupled with your experience as a professional working on projects, should allow you to focus on designing projects in such a way as to meet the expected outcomes. Keep in mind that projects are made up of teams that are responsible for some defined part of the project. A major project may have many teams.

TYPES OF PROJECTS

Projects come with different requirements related to scope, timing, cost, number of disciplines involved, various priority lists, and other variables depending on the organization's purposes. Every project within academia, government, industry, and not-for-profit organizations will have specific requirements. A product or process research project extending over many years will have different requirements than a marketing project designed to affect next year's performance. A project to provide prescription drugs through a national health program would obviously be a major project (aside from the political implications).

What kind of project are you dealing with? Any department may have projects that range from several hours to thousands of hours. Some projects may take many hours to complete, but may not require developing any new knowledge. Others could be relatively small but include many unknowns that need to be resolved. If all projects were managed with the same rigor, the output of the group could come to a standstill. However, all projects regardless of type should be tracked to prevent some minor detail from *falling through the cracks* because of a lack of attention to detail. You also need to keep in mind that most projects are made up of many subprojects managed by teams. So you need to develop a tracking system that fits the organization's needs. Chapter 4 discussed the issues related to teams.

Figure 5-1 shows some possible ways of classifying projects. For our purposes I have divided all projects into one of four groups:

❑ *Group 1* focuses on size, and uses classifications such as small to large, simple to complex, system, and macrosystem projects. A system project might include bringing a new prod-

Figure 5-1. Suggested project classification.

Group 1	Group 2	Group 3	Group 4
• Small to large • Simple to complex • System • Macrosystem	• Single discipline • Multiple disciplines	• Improvement • Routine or creative • New to organization • Breakthrough	• Scouting • New game • New business

uct to market, and will involve practically all functional groups within an organization. It might include not only building a new roadway but also solving traffic congestion. Putting a man on the moon and returning him safely was a macrosystem project. Some corporate mergers would also fit the macro class. You need to define these terms in the context of your group's and organization's purposes and objectives. What may be small or simple in one department may be large and complex in another setting.

❏ *Group 2* divides projects by single and multiple disciplines. Chances are that most single-discipline projects will require minimum effort, so that several of them may be consolidated into a single class and reported as one project. As an example, there could be a project X that collects all projects that are scheduled to take less than a certain number of hours. These projects are too small to report on individually. The multidiscipline projects usually have a much larger scope and involve significant effort.

❏ *Group 3* distinguishes projects by scope and organizational benefit. These projects usually require high levels of innovation. Process and product improvements continue to be high-priority projects in most organizations. Those improvement projects can either be routine or require high levels of creativity. Asking a group to take on the responsibility for a new-to-the-organization project usually requires some reorganization and reallocation of priorities. The breakthrough project challenges the manager to bring all the resources to bear on the project without neglecting other activities.

❑ *Group 4* projects turn attention to the future. Scouting for new or leading edge knowledge cannot be left to chance. If you consider *game* as the metaphor for *business*, you need to ask whether you are in the right game and have the right players. Those potential new business opportunities cannot be disregarded. They don't happen unless they're on the organization's agenda.

All classification systems leave something to be desired. Any project can include aspects of the individual types in Groups 1 to 4. It's possible to have a macrosystem project in Group 1 also fit into the breakthrough class in Group 3. A small project in Group 1 can also be a new-to-the-organization project in Group 3, or be the beginning of a new business in Group 4. Use your imagination and assemble any combination among the four groups or change the classification to fit your organization.

There is nothing sacred about the way projects are classified. Just make sure that you differentiate among all of them because each imposes different conditions on the group. The purpose of Figure 5-1 is to demonstrate the issues that must be considered in understanding the requirements to develop the project's purposes, objectives, and strategies. As an example, a system project will most likely be multidisciplinary, require some level of creativity, and involve some scouting. Changing the name of the business game or in your case the total operation for which you are responsible could include many selections from the groups. Such projects would be managed with much more rigor than a small single-discipline project related to some scouting activity. Every project cannot be managed in the same way. Apply the method that meets the requirements and no more.

EVALUATING PROPOSED PROJECTS

Evaluating proposed projects tests the spirit and limits of the new manager in taking on new challenges. The extent of the challenge depends on whether the proposed project falls within the discipline and experience of the manager or involves a number of unfamiliar disciplines. The challenge also depends on whether the project can be completed solely in the manager's unit or involves other groups.

It's not uncommon for a project manager to become involved in a different discipline. This is also true of small projects. Any project manager involved in developing a new product/service or making improvements or changes to an existing product/service will deal not only with technology, marketing, and sales but also with all the support functions. New disciplines and involvement of other units complicate the evaluation.

Consider the process for evaluating a project proposal submitted by some member of your department. The evaluation process as suggested here applies to all proposals that span the continuum from research to implementation of any project, related to any discipline, and in any organization be it academia, government, industry, or not-for-profit organizations. Assume that the proposal you recently received involves integrating the activities of several subunits within the organization. This complicates the evaluation process, but few proposals involve only a single subunit. What are the options?

You basically have three options: (1) scan the proposal and disregard it because you have more important priorities; (2) do a cursory review and reject it; or (3) read the proposal to gain some understanding, ask for additional clarification, and then make a decision to pursue or not pursue the effort. Choosing option 1 will send the message "Don't bother me, I have more to think about than considering something new." Such actions will stop the flow of anything that may be outside the routine day-to-day work. Option 2, the negative response, requires face-to-face discussion. You can't communicate negative decisions via e-mails or memos regardless of subject. Even though you may not support the proposal, through that face-to-face discussion you provide your reasons and show your interest in accepting unsolicited proposals.

If you choose option 3, which gives you an opportunity to ask for additional or explanatory information, you send the message that you're interested, you're available, and a very positive message of who you are; you not only talk about supporting new ideas, you welcome them. Discussions within any of the three options clarify requirements and often lead to restructuring or enhancement of the original proposal. Making decisions based solely on the written word without that face-to-face opportunity for clarifying issues often leads to forfeiting future opportunities.

The process for evaluating a proposal involves asking a series of questions that allow you to understand the scope of work and its potential for meeting the organization's established criteria for pursuing new projects. Think back to your experiences before you became a manager. Remember how many times the work had to be redone because the scope was never clearly defined, scope creep never ended, intergroup and functional requirements were never fully resolved, and the complexities of the project were never fully identified. Think about how much time was spent on rework and not only the cost but also the customer dissatisfaction that was generated in the process.

Assuming that the proposal includes the basic information required to make a decision, consider asking the following questions:

- ❏ Why should this proposal be approved and implemented?
- ❏ How does it further the interests of the organization?
- ❏ Does the proposal present something new?
- ❏ What is the value added to the organization if approved?
- ❏ What are the features, advantages, and benefits of this proposal?
- ❏ What is being offered that's really unique or special?
- ❏ What advantages will implementation of this proposal provide to the customer or the organization or society?
- ❏ Does this proposal cross national boundaries?
- ❏ What are the costs associated with implementing the proposal?
- ❏ What resources will be required from related organizational functions and are they available?
- ❏ Since the proposal offers something new, what current practices may require modification or elimination?
- ❏ What is the timeline to design what the proposal proposes, test it, go through the various stages of approval, and take it through the implementation process?
- ❏ What's the impact if the project is late?

Another approach is to consider a generic set of questions: What does the proposal accomplish? Why and why not should the organizational unit take on this challenge? How will the terms of this challenge be fulfilled? Who takes responsibility for meeting the objectives? When will this effort take place? Where will the work be done? How will performance be measured?

THE PROJECT PROCESS

The project process begins with the definition of purposes, objectives, and strategies and concludes with a postproject review.

Define the Purposes, Objectives, and Strategies

Every project begins with a clear delineation of its purposes, objectives, and strategies. I refer to these three as the up-front work that is seldom performed with sufficient diligence. Even a research project, in which there are often many unknowns, requires a description of its purposes, objectives, and strategies, although every "i" may not be dotted and every "t" may not be crossed. Since research resources are generally discretionary it becomes doubly important to allocate those resources toward some objective, preferably an objective that has a high priority for the organizational unit.

Chapter 4 included a discussion of framing in relation to teams. Keep in mind that projects are made up of teams. How you proceed with a project depends on how and to what extent you frame the project. Framing is a process by which we define the ends to be achieved, the means to achieve those ends, and the decisions to be made in the process. Framing is accomplished by beginning with fuzzy facts that are uncertain and making some sense of them. So how we frame the proposition, question, or problem makes a considerable difference. President John F. Kennedy did not describe the objective as *putting a man on the moon* but *putting a man on the moon and returning him safely by the end of the decade*. Note that this vision includes putting a man on the moon and returning him safely within a specific period of time. This vision of the effort is significantly different than if he had simply said *put a man on the moon*.

Projects such as bringing a new widget to market, restructuring the organization, providing new manufacturing facilities, changing the organization's logo, providing new financial instruments, developing wetlands, making government entities more productive, or introducing new programs to an academic institution need a well-defined statement of *purpose*. Most managers feel that their projects are fully defined, but then why do so many fail to meet expectations? In the interest of saving time, managers often fail to ask some simple questions, such as:

- ❑ What are the benefits if the project is successfully completed?
- ❑ Why are we investing resources in this project?
- ❑ What are the implications if the project does not proceed?
- ❑ Does the project fulfill the organization's vision?
- ❑ Does the project move the organization closer to what it wants to be?

Describing the project *objectives* brings us to the nitty-gritty of what we hope to accomplish. Objectives are reached through developing goals that must be reached if the objective is to be met. Every project of any significance requires a clear delineation of those goals; call them subobjectives, if you wish, but they must be defined. Too often the objectives are not fully defined, and thus begins the journey down the trail of limited resources, scope changes, and beginning of the blame game.

As an example, a project objective might be "build a house of a certain size in a specific geographic area at a particular cost." But what other factors would you need to communicate to the project manager? There are many different styles to choose from; the exterior could include many different finishes; the rooms could be large or small; the driveway might be circular or straight; and so on through many other potential choices. If you don't define those elements, the finished product will not meet your expectations. Too many projects begin with *we need to do this* without a full understanding of just what *this* includes.

Every project also requires a *strategy* for accomplishing its goals and objective. Obviously it should meet the strategic direction of the organization, but I'm referring to the strategy that will guide the project. Strategy answers the question of how: How are you going to go about meeting those objectives? What's the plan?

Agree on Preliminary Assumptions

Too often little thought is given to developing preliminary assumptions. How clearly those assumptions are delineated will determine the number of times the panic button will be pushed. You need to document the known and unknown, the controllable and uncontrollable, and the predictable and unpredictable. The unknown, the unpredictable, and the uncontrollable must be rationalized now; it is very easy to disregard these three "UNs" until later stages of the project. The time to begin working on them is *now*.

Laissez-faire project management doesn't work. You can't make up the game as you go along. People need a modus operandi, especially if a large number of players are involved. The best results are achieved when everyone plays from the same sheet of music. Keep in mind that as new information becomes available changes in direction may be required. The project team must be able to accept these changes.

Conduct the Required Study

Most projects require some research or study that adds new information. If no new information is required, you might question the necessity of pursuing the project: just more of the same may not provide any competitive advantage. There are competitors who will challenge the best and the brightest. Those challenges require a response. The question usually revolves around how much research or study is necessary. Too little information may not provide an acceptable approach and too much information can be costly and time consuming without providing any appreciable benefit.

Reexamine Preliminary Assumptions

As the project progresses, take the time to reevaluate those preliminary assumptions. You need the full team to do a proper evaluation since you will probably not be current on the requirements of each discipline that's involved. Unfortunately and too often, any information that somehow contradicts the basic assumptions will be greeted with much skepticism. Plans were based on those preliminary assumptions but plans are not cast in bronze; they're a guide to achieve a result and should be modified when necessary.

Identify Alternative Solutions

Taking time to evaluate alternative solutions can pay big dividends, but deciding how many to consider is a judgment call. It takes more time to evaluate alternative solutions, but the process provides a high degree of confidence. It's easy to apply a quick fix without any consideration of the system or future needs. You need to keep in mind that there is seldom a perfect solution; there is only the most appropriate one from a group of possible solutions that can be implemented through the available resources and infrastructure. Identifying alternatives also involves estimating the results from each solution. While financial results are the easiest to measure, they may not always lead to the right choice. Those nonquantifiable issues of each alternative require consideration. That calls for judgment.

Select the Solution

There is no prescriptive method for selecting the appropriate solution. Some simple questions can be asked:

❏ Is the solution realizable within the organization's financial and structural limitations?

❏ Does the solution meet all of the project requirements?

❏ Does the solution provide for use in pursuing future opportunities?

❏ Does the solution leverage the current bank of the organization's proprietary knowledge?

❏ Is the required level of expertise available within or outside the organization?

❏ Is there a project manager available with the required credentials, experience, and track record?

These are basic questions and need to be expanded based on the project's scope and importance to the organization.

Define Resources, Cost, and Timeline

Projects succeed or fail depending on the available resources, the accuracy of cost projections, and a realizable timeline. As a rule we don't do a very good job of defining project resources; too little emphasis is placed on track record and too much on academic credentials. I suggest that educational background be given secondary consideration for any person who has been out of school for more than five years. There must be a balance, and the track record should take precedence.

Estimating project cost creates difficulties for most people. Yet the costs determine the viability of the project. It's very difficult for a manager to identify all costs without the help of the group. But group members are often reluctant to commit to some fixed number of hours because they'll be expected to meet their commitment. Organizations differ on how cost projections are made. Generally for major projects, the project manager will develop those costs with considerable assistance from the accounting department or the subunit's assigned controller.

After the timeline is presented to upper-level management, the response may be: *that's not good enough*; *we need the project completed within the next twelve months*. A give-and-take discussion follows: it can't be done, why not, what do you need to meet the twelve-month schedule, and so on. Eventually, an agreement is reached but in too many cases the timeline is unrealistic. This is why *we never have enough time to do it the right way but plenty of time to do it over*. Timelines must be realistic and can usually be met by modestly limiting the initial scope of the project without seriously limiting the expectations.

Work Breakdown Structure

Technology-oriented departments are familiar with work breakdown structure but administrative and distribution functions seldom use it. Very simply, work breakdown structure divides the project work into many tasks. This provides a way for understanding the pieces and also understanding how those pieces must come together and at what time. The work breakdown structure also puts the tasks in some order for completion and develops priorities. There is a tendency to focus early attention on what's known rather than on resolving the unknown issues.

Estimate Cost/Benefit

While project cost is important, estimating the cost/benefit of the solution is of equal if not greater importance. The benefits to be derived from the investment of resources determine whether the project will gain approval. Organizations generally use some form of cost/benefit analysis for approving projects: payback period, net present value (NPV), return on investment (ROI), and modified forms of each of these. They are tailor-made to the organization and also include some minimum hurdle rate for approval. For projects that have no direct financial benefit, some sort of cost/benefit analysis must still be developed.

Consider this example: the human resource department suggests introducing a new performance appraisal system. The costs can be developed without any difficulty, but the benefits are difficult to measure if required to meet some financial hurdle rate. Those costs basically include the time required to accomplish the appraisal process, and since new appraisals usually become more complex and are done more often, they require more time, which can add considerable cost.

Evaluate the Risk

Every project requires an evaluation of the risk involved. Success is not guaranteed regardless of the effort put forth in diligently developing the background information. There is a difference between managing the uncertainties and evaluating risks. Uncertainties include that complete list of unknown and unpredictable issues. Resolution of the unknowns can be accommodated, but the unpredictable elements need to be addressed throughout the whole project. The level of these uncertainties determines the risks that must be evaluated in relation to the organization's ability to accept the risk.

Prepare an Implementation Program

Implementation plans must meet the needs of the project. Some may be very simple and others complex, but all must be straightforward and direct. They may be extensive in detail, but the detail should follow to a logical conclusion without any gaps. The what, the when, the where, the how, and by whom must be answered.

Managing the Project Processes

Once the project has been approved and work begun, there are activities that need to be reevaluated frequently throughout the life of the project. All the data accumulated during the project approval stage needs to be under constant evaluation. New competitors may have entered the field; new technologies may have surfaced; new markets may have become apparent; new government regulations may have been imposed; budgets may have been reduced; and the organization's direction may have also changed.

Continue Evaluating Priorities

Priorities will change during a project because what may have been considered as a known becomes an unknown. New information was uncovered that needs to be addressed. Certain tasks were initially defined, and in the process of completing those tasks the original assumptions were invalidated. You need to go back to the drawing board, so to speak, to find a new solution if the project is to meet its time schedule. Also events and tasks that are listed as predictable often prove to be unpredictable and troublesome because other expected results were not achieved.

Control Scope Creep

Scope creep involves adding features to a project after it has been approved; it is one of the major issues that prevent organizations from completing projects within specification, on time, and at estimated cost. At the very least scope creep increases cost, often requires time-consuming rework, deprives other value-adding projects of resources, delays the launch of the project's output, and can cause a loss of major business opportunities. But scope creep will always be with you and you need to find ways of controlling it. The amount of scope creep depends on the rigor that was applied during the stages prior to management approval. Well-conceived projects should not require any major changes in scope, but you need to recognize that perfection is not attainable, so there will inevitably be some changes that will have to be implemented.

Control the Documentation

Not very many people care to update the project's documentation. Let's face it, it's a boring job, it doesn't require any creativity or innovation or personal initiative, and yet it plays a major role in determining future actions. The past history is important both from the managing and operational perspective. Documentation covers all functions and disciplines. There is no excuse for sloppy documentation. Just think back over your years as a professional and calculate the lost hours because prior work wasn't properly documented. Proper documentation involves keeping a running history of the project and documenting events, changes in direction and scope, and modifying plans as required.

Project Reviews

Project reviews are not a matter of choice, especially when the project involves several disciplines and departments. Regardless of their high levels of competence and dedication, people must be brought together in some type of forum to review the project status. Those pieces of the puzzle must fit into the right places. There may be misunderstandings of the requirements that need to be clarified. There may be conflicts in design parameters. New information may have been uncovered that requires changes. Unless these problems are corrected in a timely manner, much of the work effort can become useless.

The greatest pitfall of all project reviews is a lack of candor about the real situation. Those formal presentations often fail to tell the complete story. We are all aware of projects that are on schedule for a year or more and in the last week require additional months to complete. Every review must focus attention on the knockouts, which are those items that if not resolved in a timely manner will in essence scuttle the project. They must be identified and resources provided to resolve them. Wishful thinking will not provide the answers.

The project manager takes total responsibility for the project and needs firsthand information about the status. Depending solely on project reviews really doesn't work. Making decisions solely from those written reports and checking the latest project management computer program isn't enough. Project managers need to get into the act without micromanaging. There's only one way to determine the status of a project: do your own investigation. That doesn't imply that you don't trust your people, it means you want to know what's going on.

Whom you appoint as a project manager does make a difference. The project manager should have some understanding of the disciplines involved in the project; not necessary at the expert level, but some understanding. At a project management conference I met with a group of software developers for a general discussion of project management issues. The session quickly deteriorated into a criticism of their project managers. This was the first time I had heard such vociferous criticism of project managers. After much discussion of the issues I focused attention on the background of the project managers. All but one was a recent MBA graduate without any understanding of software development, which is not a very good set of credentials for a software project manager. It's important that project managers understand what they're managing.

Develop a Project Control System

How much project control do you need? Just enough; not too much, not too little. Forget about the war room approach with all the graphs and data. Much of the reporting is irrelevant. A project is made up of a series of tasks derived from the work breakdown structure that are assigned to a specific individual or group. Each of these tasks has a specific requirement, a completion date, and a cost. So there are basically three factors to track. The status of each task against its goal is a judgment call; you're not counting widgets coming off the production line. You're looking at the results of the thinking that has taken place in order to resolve some specific issue that can't be quantified by some algorithm. The cost data is quantifiable and useful if presented in a timely manner and includes all associated costs. The schedule is quantifiable; you either have or have not met the expectations as originally defined for some point in time. There are no "almost yes" answers, only "yes" or "no." A "no" answer requires a statement of the problem and a means for resolving it.

There are many project management software programs available for project control. The challenge lies in determining which one fits your requirements. My comments are not made to set you against computerized project planning and monitoring, but to help you avoid the necessity of dedicating a full-time person to manage the program and develop data that provides little if any benefit. So while the choice of program is important, it is only a means to some end; it is not an end in itself. It's a tool to help manage projects more effectively.

Some project management programs are merely scheduling programs. Others go into extensive detail, providing tools for team selection, tracking start and finish dates of each task, hours required from each individual, automatically updating the complete program in the event of some missed target date, identifying direct and overhead costs, requesting information based on prior considerations, and an array of issues that may or may not be necessary for your particular group. The question always remains: What information do you and your project managers need to manage your projects? There is no one program that fits all situations and data should only be generated if the data adds value in some way.

Postproject Review

The value of a postproject review, or postmortem as some choose to call it, cannot be overemphasized. It provides an opportunity to assess the overall quality of the project effort. But the review is only valuable if issues, those having either a positive or negative impact, are brought to the surface and discussed openly. Positive performance issues may be subsequently designated as best practices. Dealing with the negative aspects of the project presents greater difficulty. The discussion cannot deal with personnel issues; that discussion if necessary should be done in private. The group should be asking two simple questions: What did we do well? What did we do not so well?

Questions may relate to the clarity of the project statement, the description of the goals and objectives, the planning process, the work breakdown structure, the use of resources, the communication system, the information system, the original schedule and cost estimate, the changes in scope, the project management system, timely decision making, and any related issues. This exercise is not done to post a grade but to learn from the experience and in the future take advantage of the positive practices and try and eliminate the negative practices.

MULTIFUNCTIONAL PROJECTS

Multifunctional projects present a new set of problems for the new manager. Multifunctional projects involve bringing functional units together, such as marketing and public relations, engineering and accounting, legal and safety with manufacturing, and any combination of two or more of the organization's functional units. The complexity comes from the need to involve the managers from each of these units: excellent conditions for beginning the turf wars.

Project managers live in a world characterized by conflict. Human nature being what it is, functional managers vie for position. They often protect their own turf to the exclusion of working for the benefit of the whole organization. They fight for resources, for leadership, and for clients (clients defined broadly as anyone either internally or externally who might seek their services). They try to balance client needs versus organizational needs. How do you manage these conflicts?

When conflicts arise someone must step forward and make the decision. Democratic management doesn't work when two immovable objects face each other. A lifetime on bread and water would not move these people from their positions. Multifunctional conflicts in which you as a manager are involved with other managers must go to the next level of management. Turf battles waste time and precious resources. There may be times when upper management has no alternative and must make a decision to either relocate or dismiss functional managers who cannot function as part of a team.

MANAGING PROJECTS ACROSS CULTURES

As a new manager you may become involved in projects that cross national boundaries with significantly different cultures. The history of managing projects involving different cultures does not present a very favorable picture. Fortunately there has been some improvement. Within the last couple of decades American industry realized that it did not have all the answers; those people across either ocean had excellent ideas and were able to match wits with our best and brightest. In reality managing projects across cultures is about people. As I noted in the early part of this book, managers do not manage people; they manage the activities of people. That is the first step toward developing working relationships in other cultures. You do not manage people; you manage their activities.

Managing across borders involves knowing the people you're working with. While organizations recognize this as a need in their own country, they somehow conclude that getting people together face-to-face when other cultures are involved may not be necessary. It's important that you know something about the person on the other end of that telephone line or that e-mail. You can't manage cross-cultural projects if you don't know the people and the culture.

Language is generally the greatest barrier. It takes a great deal of patience, especially when language fluency in each other's language is lacking. Working with translators provides one way but much depends on the competence of the translator. While giving some lectures in Bulgaria in English, my comments were translated into Bulgarian by an interpreter. I noticed during my presentation that I wasn't receiving the kind of feedback from the audience that I had expected. During the break I asked my host, who spoke excellent English, whether or not the translator was editorializing. A definite yes. The interpreter was providing his own spin. We discussed the issue with the translator and while the situation improved it was less than satisfactory. The next day I was provided with a new translator who really functioned as a translator.

Having spent many years working in Europe I found that on major projects it's possible to develop a project culture that somehow transcends two cultures, or even three or more cultures if necessary. It takes a project manager who is sensitive to the cultural issues, makes at least an attempt to learn some of the language, and more importantly learns something about the history of the countries involved. The project manager doesn't need to be dominated by a new culture. Don't waste time on the nonessential. If certain formalities or protocols exist, follow them unless they're detrimental in some way to the project. Focus on the work at hand and on managing activities.

STRATEGIC PROJECT MANAGEMENT

There is a strategic component of project management that cannot be disregarded. A project may meet the functional requirements, the projected schedule, and the cost projections, but what does it actually do for the organization? What is the value added from this effort, not just to your department, but also in meeting the organization's objectives? Even though the project may have been justified financially, what was the net benefit to the organization? If the project was justified by some qualitative data, what was the benefit to the organization? Some projects will be approved because they must be accomplished and there may not be a quantitative or qualitative justification, but the benefits must be defined in terms of the total organization.

Dr. Aaron J. Shenhar suggested that the current dynamic business environment requires taking a strategic approach to project management.[1] Although Shenhar's research was directed to technology managers, it applies to all organizations regardless of discipline. The strategic framework of project management focuses on creating competitive advantage rather than just meeting the immediate requirements. This strategic approach applies to academia, government, industry, and not-for-profit organizations.

You ask how competitive advantage applies to academia, government, and the not-for-profit world. Academic institutions compete with one another, there is competition within government for funding projects, and not-for-profit organizations must split a limited pool of money. Today, more than ever, these organizations need to dedicate their limited resources to projects that make a difference, not just projects that may be interesting to explore.

Strategy is often discussed in broad and somewhat vague terms. Too often strategy includes plans and actions and decisions to achieve specific outcomes. Too often strategic directions are wishes without benefit of resources and appropriate management infrastructure. In simple terms *project strategy involves a project perspective, direction, and guidelines on what to do and how to do it to achieve the best results.* Shenhar's approach to strategic project management relies on six basic principles:

1. *Leadership.* The project manager takes total responsibility for results. If the project involves the introduction of a new prod-

uct the project manager's responsibility ends when the customer is satisfied. A project manager's responsibility for a research study on any topic in any organization ends when the final decision is made as to the findings of the research.

2. *Strategy.* Define the competitive advantage of the product, process, or service and articulate a winning strategy; determine what it will take and how it will be accomplished.

3. *Spirit.* What to do and how to do it must be described in the context of what the organization wants to be—the vision. That vision expresses the value of the effort.

4. *Adaptation.* All projects are not the same. Managers need to assess, classify, and adapt their project management style to the project requirements. The style will be different if the project crosses national boundaries. The style and practices will be quite different for a project including only a few people. The assessment process should vary by orders of magnitude in each of these situations. Each presents different levels of uncertainty, complexity, and pace.

5. *Integration.* Sometimes every activity has been completed as expected, yet the system doesn't function. Sometimes every participant made major contributions, worked diligently, and met the required expectations, and yet the system under consideration failed. Why? Probably because all the activities weren't adequately integrated. Don't lose sight of the fact that the devil is in the details.

6. *Learning.* Organizations will have a difficult time meeting expectations if everyone must begin the project management journey at the bottom of the learning curve. Organizational learning is a continual process of recording and publicizing the *new* that has been learned and then summarizing it into an easily accessible database. Organizations are doomed to repeat the same mistakes if they don't develop some sort of mechanism to capture the learning that occurred.

Shenhar's strategic approach takes a broader look at project management. It asks the question: If this project meets all of its requirements, what does it really do for the organization? What are the real benefits? You have probably worked on projects as a professional that had no impact on the organization. Your management may have considered it a success because you met all the requirements, but it really didn't add any value to the organization.

SUMMARY

❑ Project design determines the probability of success. Yes, some haphazard projects have been successful, but the vast majority—even if successful—seldom make effective use of the organization's resources.

❑ Develop a system for classifying projects. Not all projects require the same amount of attention to detail. The classification sends the message as to the project's importance. The project process requires following a structure that fits the organization's needs. Those many steps in the process require thinking about the consequences of each step rather than just following a series of actions.

❑ Many projects involve multifunctional effort. The project manager's challenge involves integrating these group activities.

❑ Managing projects across cultures requires sensitivity to customs and protocols but not domination by them. Focus on managing activities.

❑ When organizations focus on improving effectiveness and efficiency, project activities must focus on adding value to the organization.

NOTE

1. Aaron Shenhar, "Project Management: A Strategic Approach," Institute of Electrical and Electronics Engineers (IEEE), *Engineering Management Society Newsletter* 50, 4 (1999): 6–11.

CHAPTER 6

Finding the Time and Doing the Work

Most people today claim to be overworked. The media's descriptions of managers and professionals who work anywhere from sixty to one hundred hours per week reinforce an impression that may or may not be true. The business and public press add to this dilemma by continually raising the issues of worker stress and its impact on family life and society. I have always observed how people work; from the waiter who presents the menu, takes the order, serves the meal, and clears the table to the way specialists, managers, and senior executives work. I suggest that the majority of overwork stems from the many *make-work activities* imposed by all levels of management, lack of knowledge to work effectively and efficiently, the failure of managers to delegate nonessential activities (all those activities beneath their pay level), and the inability to reach decisions in a timely manner. You don't need a software program to find out where you're spending your time. All you need is pencil and paper.

OVERWORKED

Why and how often do you spend evenings and weekends doing work that should have been done during regular working hours? When you work at professional and management levels, you accept the fact that at times the extra effort will be required. But how often is this necessary? If this situation begins blurring the lines between personal and work life you need to take a good hard look at what you're doing and how you're doing it. Downsizing is often blamed for much of this overwork. There is no doubt that downsizing has in some cases added more work for some people, but how much of it is necessary? Were these discharged people fully occupied and was their work effort adding value?

Welch et al.[1] describe overwork as a subjective phenomenon that is different from the actual number of hours worked. Although people feel they are working longer hours, the research is not clear. One research effort claims that people are working 163 more hours per year than they did in the 1960s. Another survey showed that employees were working 140 fewer hours than in the 1960s. Those people who now as a matter of rule work 60 or more hours per week would disagree. So what factors give these impressions of additional worked hours? Recognizing that research in this area is very complex, here are some general conclusions reached by Welch et al.:

❑ Work and personal life are more integrated because of technology. People feel they never leave work. The cell phone needs to be answered 24/7. Or does it?

❑ Leisure time is more fragmented and taken in shorter segments, giving the impression that people don't have sufficient time to actually relax.

❑ Employed parents with young children feel overworked because of time demands at home and at work.

❑ The impact of empowerment on the perception of overwork depends on how empowerment programs work. The organizational culture, structure, and processes need to be changed to accommodate empowerment, otherwise it is viewed as additional work.

Another overwork factor that is not mentioned above involves what people do with their personal time and how their personal activities have changed over the last three or four decades. Do you ever wonder how those venues related to sports, the arts, travel, advanced education, and other social engagements have placed additional demands on your personal time? The Sunday picnic is no longer a big event. The tailgate sports events that begin at 8:00 A.M. or before and continue through 5:00 P.M. or later take the whole day.

Are people overworked? I suggest that, with the exception of specific instances when they've made a commitment and want to fulfill that commitment to maintain their reputation, continuous overwork can be reduced considerably if not eliminated. But while it takes a commitment on the part of executive management to send the message that make-work reduces effectiveness, you as the manager can control the make-work in your department through your managing practices.

Some research suggests that the answer to resolving the overwork issue involves giving employees more choice and flexibility over when and how they work. I suggest that perhaps developing some organizational discipline may be more helpful. By instilling discipline I don't mean that managers begin browbeating employees. I do suggest that managers set appropriate performance standards, allow for flexibility where and when required, and make sure that employees abide by them. As an example, flexible scheduling (flextime) gave employees more control over work hours and has been a moderate success for employees but at the cost of lost work hours for the organization. Introduction of technology into the workplace has also met with questionable results. So let's look at some of the time wasters for you as the manager and those that you impose on others.

WHO'S GOT THE MONKEY?

Oncken and Wass[2] in their article "Management Time: Who's Got the Monkey?" asked: "Why is it that managers are typically running out of time while their subordinates are typically running out of work?" This question may be difficult to answer since it seems that many professionals and their managers consider themselves to be overworked in some way.

Of course some may consider the question irrelevant. The authors ask a few simple but important questions. Do you as a manager really need to be involved? Do you need to accept all these monkeys thrust on your back by your subordinates? Why do you accept responsibility to provide subordinates with information? Why don't you just reverse the process and give the responsibility to the subordinate? You're expected to delegate, so why don't you delegate? Do you allow subordinates to place additional responsibilities on your shoulders?

The answers include a range of responses: insecurity in making decisions; prestige if the question involves acquiring information from upper management; the desire to micromanage; the inability to accept responsibility for the actions of others; and a subordinate, by taking initiative, may make you look like a wimp. The authors refer to these subordinate-imposed responsibilities as *monkeys*.

Oncken and Wass present five hard-and-fast rules for the "care and feeding of monkeys":

❏ *Rule 1*. Monkeys should be fed or shot. Otherwise managers will waste valuable resources.

❏ *Rule 2*. The monkey population should be kept below the maximum number the manager has time to feed.

❏ *Rule 3*. Monkeys should be fed by appointment only.

❏ *Rule 4*. Monkeys should be fed face-to-face or by telephone, but never by mail.

❏ *Rule 5*. Every monkey should have an assigned next feeding time and degree of initiative.

From my years of experience I propose a few additional rules:

❏ *Rule 6*. Subordinates who deliver too many monkeys may need a change of environment. So find the problem. Maybe these subordinates think they can survive on monkey business.

❏ *Rule 7*. Monkeys must present everything in writing. This exercise forces them to think before asking you to do the thinking for them.

❏ **Rule 8**. Don't attach yourself to monkeys in the elevator or at social occasions.

What does a manager do with these people who like to raise monkeys? There are two answers, but only one really helps you recoup your investment in people: If they are educable, then educate them to meet your expectations; if not, find them a different cage or send them back to the wild.

GOING BEYOND THE MONKEYS

In economic climates in which organizations are attempting to do more with less, many managers and professionals conclude that executive management is doing nothing more than passing on the workload of the furloughed to those who remain. That's where the additional work hours come from. That may or may not be true depending on whether or not all the furloughed people had a full workload. Downsizing is all the more reason to evaluate, to analyze, to prioritize, to eliminate what no longer adds value, and then focus on the priority issues. While managing your time is important, I believe the greater benefit comes from finding the sources of lost time and eliminating them.

Somewhere along the line many managers and professionals either never learned how to work effectively and efficiently or forgot *how to work*. They disregard the impact of lost time on performance. An hour of lost time per day by each employee represents 12.5 percent of the traditional eight-hour workday. Lost time occurs in many different places and as a result of inaction or some improper action. Oncken and Wass described boss-imposed time, system-imposed time, and self-imposed time. But the origins of lost time go beyond these three categories. Consider the following lost-time generators.

❏ Lost time imposed from the top of the organization
❏ Lost time imposed by the system
❏ Lost time imposed by managers
❏ Lost time within the functional silos

❑ Lost time from meeting mania

❑ Time frittered away by people

❑ External lost time generators

LOST TIME IMPOSED FROM THE TOP OF THE ORGANIZATION

Creating lost time begins with the CEO and upper management and its various committees. Lost time is generated throughout the organization when various directives are communicated without full consideration of the impact of the directive. As an example, a directive stated that on a particular date an organization would institute flexible hours. In this case the program included a modified version of the time clock: all staff members would punch in and punch out, except they would do it electronically at the office. The program also included compensatory time for professionals at the end of the month for all hours worked over 40 hours per week. Unfortunately, the directive did not provide for a way to "punch in" remotely. Thus employees who traveled as part of their job now had to go to their office, sign in, begin their travel, go about their daily business, return in the evening, and sign out. As a result, eight-hour days now stretched to ten or more hours, with a resulting increase in compensatory time. This does not argue against flexible hours, but shows the need to consider all the potential problems before implementing such a sweeping new policy.

Delays in decisions by top management consume hours of discussion as the information flows down through the organization. The hours lost by merely discussing the lack of decision multiply geometrically from the top to the bottom of the organization. The major problem arises when it takes top management more time to make the decision than to implement the proposed work; the clock is running and time is wasted. Each iteration of a proposal followed with requests for more information is usually a delaying tactic that not only wastes the time associated with the preparation but the grumbling time of those who need to make one more pass.

So what can you do as a newly appointed manager about these directives and delays in making decisions? Not much, if anything at all. But you can be sensitive to these issues and know when to cut off the discussion among your people. The directive was given and the decision was delayed, so get on with the other work of your group.

LOST TIME IMPOSED BY THE SYSTEM

Any grouping of individuals assembled for some business purpose is governed by four major interactive requirements: a lean organizational design; some guiding principles; a limited number of policies and procedures; and recommended practices. Each of these four requirements, individually and collectively, impose conditions on the system that can, if not controlled, generate work that does not add value.

Organizational Design

Organizational design generates lost time when too many interfaces become involved in any transaction and too many people are involved in the decision loop; the more people involved in the decision process, the greater the opportunity for generating lost time. As more professional disciplines, more functions, and more departments become involved in the decision process, it becomes more difficult to rationalize the redundancies and reach a decision without excessive hours of discussion.

In expanding economies, organizations add people without as much rigorous evaluation of future needs. Projects are added without the necessary evaluation and current projects continue even if they have a low potential for adding value. It's not difficult to be successful when the economy is on an up cycle and all systems are "go" and meeting their objectives. But there comes a time when the economy declines and requires a reduction in staff. Such situations generate countless hours of lost time, not only at the time the staff is reduced but also in debating the future viability of the department or organization.

The usual response to added workload is: If we're going to take on this new project, we need more people. But added staff may not be the answer. Why not consider the complete project load and eliminate those tasks that have the least or perhaps no impact on the organization's performance or may no longer need to be completed? Just ask: Why are we working on this project? What are the benefits? If eliminating certain projects has no negative impact on the department or the organization, why pursue them?

You have most likely heard about building a "lean and mean organization." Lean and mean really doesn't work. Lean, yes; mean, no. Lean and managerially disciplined provides a more responsible approach for the organization and its employees.

Guiding Principles

Guiding principles usually define how the organization will function. They define the organization's philosophy of operation. But as a manager you will also develop an operating philosophy; that philosophy will most likely have your stamp on it. That philosophy will define your style and your expectations. That philosophy will define you as a manager. Will you be proactive? Will you foster creativity and innovation? Will you be receptive to new ideas? Will you go out on a limb to protect an employee? Will you treat everyone with respect? This list of questions is endless and depends on the purpose of your department. Your philosophy will also most likely reflect the organizational philosophy to a greater or lesser extent.

But guiding principles can also become stumbling blocks. The educators suggest that principles need to be internalized, but for how long? IBM fostered a policy of *taking care* of its employees, but did they carry it too far? In the early 1990s IBM's CEOs were complaining that employees had become too comfortable. Who allowed them to become comfortable? Where were the CEOs in the 1980s when it all began? You can't argue about taking care of employees, but you can go too far. IBM eventually reduced its total employment from a peak of 407,000 in 1986 to 325,000 in 1992. As time went on, IBM made further reductions in total employees. Principles and processes that are internalized must be reviewed periodically to determine if the foundations of those principles maintain legitimacy.

Throughout this book I have promoted the idea of managers being proactive as a guiding management principle. But being proactive does not suggest keeping your organization in turmoil with a new flavor of the day. One program needs to be digested before another is presented. Being proactive involves being productive. You can't emphasize creativity and innovation verbally and then fail to provide the required resources or infrastructure. You can't continually seek new ideas without focusing on completing the work at hand. If you're a proactive manager you will go out on a limb to support your employees rather than turn the decision over to the bureaucracy. These are the high-anxiety activities. Respect for the individual cannot be compromised. Each of these questions requires balancing the needs of the group and the individual. Principles must let the department members know where you're taking the group and what it wants to be. The message must be clear and cannot change every time some new crisis arises.

Policies and Procedures

Policies and procedures (P&P) were introduced at one time to develop standards of operation. Everyone didn't have to start at the bottom of the learning curve. But like many things P&P went amok. Too often they include thousands of pages of minutiae that created a bureaucracy determined to make sure they're fully enforced. P&Ps are essential, but when they hinder performance they need to be either modified or discontinued. Unfortunately the people who write the policies and procedures seldom have to implement them. They also write them with little or no input from the implementers. Policies cover human resources, technology, quality, intellectual property, and continuing education, as well as many other activities, often right down to how to purchase a pencil. Procedures describe the process by which certain activities are performed and can help or hinder performance. But procedures cannot be so prescriptive that they do not make allowances for personal judgment. Responsibility and accountability for actions cannot be dictated. Managers who focus on delivering results will find ways to circumvent restrictive procedures that prevent reaching objectives. These system-imposed time wasters need to be controlled. You need to question all procedures and reduce them to a minimum. While you may be concerned about the organization's P&Ps you must be cautious about adding restrictive policies and procedures for your department.

Recommended Practices

Recommended practices arise from benchmarking processes from within and outside the organization. The purpose is to avoid reinventing the wheel. If some process has provided significant benefits in some department, can that same process be duplicated in other departments? Although the recommended practices are less restrictive than procedures, they cannot be allowed to hinder progress. What may work in one department may not work in another, even though conditions are similar. However, the benchmarking process cannot become an end unto itself. Benchmarking only provides a benefit if its application adds value in some way. It may be more appropriate to take the time and develop the next-generation process than depend on what has become common property and provides no competitive advantage.

LOST TIME IMPOSED BY MANAGERS

Managers at all levels contribute to lost time and often do not recognize the implications on performance. The lists of activities that consume employees' time and add little or no value are endless. Here are some examples: requiring excessive planning activities that disregard the effectiveness and efficiency with which the plans are implemented; introducing new panaceas for improving performance without sufficient knowledge; using benchmarking instead of being the leaders in the field; continually changing priorities; neglecting to provide consistent feedback, which leads to speculation about the unknown and generates the rumor mill; disregarding the importance of thinking before doing; and taking a myopic or narrow view rather than looking at the impact on the system. Your experiences will allow you to add your own time wasters to this list.

LOST TIME WITHIN THE FUNCTIONAL SILOS

Functional units generate additional lost time because of the way they work: they protect their kingdoms. Each function operates independently without much regard for other functions. By focusing solely on their own interests they limit the opportunities for building a dynamic and sustainable organization. Success involves integrating all of these independent silos.

❏ Researchers work at their own pace; they are very methodical, and take a step-by-step approach. They're not amenable to doing the last experiment first. The output from research is useless unless somehow transformed into products or services.

❏ If product development is isolated from research activities until the research is completed, then much rework will be required. These two groups must be engaged in each other's activities early in the introduction of a new product or process.

❏ The manufacturing silo is the last stop before a product or service goes to the customer. One out of tolerance component can prevent a product from meeting the user's expectations. One lost bit of information can make a computer program fail. These failures create lost time.

❏ Marketing and sales live in the real world. All the effort up to this point is useless if the customer doesn't buy. Investments in new products and services that do not meet the customer's requirements generate lost time.

❏ Physical distribution receives very little attention until the telephone rings and a customer complains about a missing or late delivery. Tracking down lost items, following up on late deliveries, and dealing with the interruptions adds to the lost time in physical distribution. Additional lost time may come from time required by order entry and processing, billing, and any related functions.

❏ Customer service involves pre- and post-sales activities. The process begins when the product is sold and ends when the customer is satisfied with the performance. Time spent attempting to quiet an irate customer because of lack of product performance adds to the lost time report.

❏ Financial silos are not generally well versed about the research, product development, and other functional silos. The reverse is also true. But how many times are you going to rework the financial part of a proposal? Every added iteration adds more lost time.

❑ Human resource departments may not be directly involved in the idea to product cycle but they are a source of lost time. For example, evaluating individual performance has become overcomplicated and the added complexity provides little value for the required effort. Evaluation involves judgment and always will.

LOST TIME FROM MEETING MANIA

Meetings consume a disproportionate amount of every employee's available work hours and contribute to lost time. Meetings are required but they need to be managed. In most situations too many people are asked to attend, the meetings become a forum for pushing an agenda, and too often the concerns that led to the meeting being called are not resolved. While it is necessary to get people involved, to keep them informed, and also give them an opportunity to provide input, it is also necessary to find ways of satisfying these requirements without excessive waste of time.

As a manager you will probably participate in many meetings regarding your department's activities and other organizational meetings. While you may not be able to control or shape the organizational meetings, you can design your department's meetings to be effective and efficient. There are no mysteries to managing meetings. The requirements are simple:

❑ Define the purpose of the meeting.
❑ Develop the agenda but leave room for flexibility.
❑ Identify any specific preparation that participants need. (Don't keep plowing the same ground over and over.)
❑ Include only the participants who can contribute or have a need to know.
❑ Engage in a dialogue rather than discussion.
❑ Focus on facts and their justification.
❑ Bring all the critical issues out in the open.
❑ Make the required decisions based on available resources.
❑ Prepare a list of action items with assignments and schedule.

❑ Document the results of the meeting.

❑ Communicate the results to all who have a need to know.

Recognize the fact that meetings will be called on the spur of the moment without the time to go through this series of formal steps. Although the requirements may not be written down and passed out ahead of the scheduled meeting, following the steps allows for a more disciplined process and reduces the time required for the meeting.

TIME FRITTERED AWAY BY PEOPLE

At one time executives were concerned about employees using the organization's telephone system for personal calls except when absolutely necessary. They wondered how many pencils were being used for personal use. They were also concerned about the time spent by the water cooler before the days of multiple side-by-side food dispensers. Today's executives are concerned about the amount of organizational time spent on personal e-mail and Web searches. Studies show that an average of one hour per day is lost on personal e-mails or personal Internet use. Whether it's an hour or a half-hour per day is irrelevant; it's lost time, and when multiplied by the number of employees, the figure takes on real significance. Can you imagine an organization of 10,000 people losing 10,000 working hours per day? It happens very easily.

Everyone in the organization fritters time away, starting right at the top. We will never achieve 100 percent utilization of our time. No one can be productive for 480 minutes in a 480-minute day. There's a certain amount of socialization that is essential, even though it doesn't directly add to productivity. Much of the frittered-away time is due to lack of discipline, but discipline is not defined as conformance, strictness, punishment, or being tough or mean. Discipline involves a balance of order and freedom to act; it establishes limits of acceptable performance and provides for continuous improvement; it engenders an environment and a spirit where personal commitments will be met; it allows no excuses.

Those directives coming from the top of the pyramid and from all functional executives can either improve performance or hinder it. Too often these requests generate make-work without any possibility of improving performance. They usually occur when some guru or academic develops a new program that will take the organization "to the next level." Unfortunately focusing solely on such issues as empowerment, reengineering the organization, participative management, and all the other single-issue fads doesn't guarantee success.

Those routine reports demanded by all levels consume inordinate amounts of time. Many are seldom read and generally end up in some archive. As a manager you will most likely be expected to provide inputs to your own manager. You do have an opportunity to either eliminate those reports totally or restructure them so they don't require as much effort. It may take some selling skills but it's your department that's frittering away the time.

In my first supervisory position, managing fourteen engineers, I found that there was too much time spent writing monthly reports on every project. There were eight supervisors reporting to one manager, and the complete department included about 150 engineers, designers, and draftsmen. The eight supervisors provided special high-technology engineering services to about thirty other managers. Keep in mind this was when personal computers with Microsoft Word were only a dream, so every report had to be typed. I approached my manager, who was one of about fifteen managers reporting to the director of engineering, and suggested that we provide formal monthly reports only for projects over a certain value. This would eliminate about 85 percent of the effort being devoted to generating reports. I was told that this was impossible. I continued to raise the issue at our monthly meetings, and my manager finally agreed that we could try it.

So we stopped the formal reporting procedure on all projects below a certain dollar amount. We heard no comment from the thirty managers that we served. Eight months later the director of engineering approached my manager and said he had not received the monthly department report. The manager politely informed him that we discontinued it eight months ago. The director responded with a few very unpleasant words but that was the end of the small project report. How many hours had been wasted over the years to write and distribute those reports that nobody read or at least found essential for meeting their objectives?

EXTERNAL LOST-TIME GENERATORS

External relations influence the time lost in each of the lost-time categories. Every organization deals with special interest groups to a greater or lesser extent. Some customers may be troublesome and tiresome but they need to be dealt with; they cannot be ignored. Suppliers can be both an asset and a liability; if they meet their commitments, they are assets, but if they do not meet their commitments then they can consume inordinate amounts of time to resolve issues.

Governmental agencies from the lowest to the highest reduce time for productive work by requesting services from organizations. The J. Peter Grace report issued on *Federal Government Cost Control*[3] involved 36 task forces, 161 corporate executives, 2,000 volunteers, and provided 2,478 separate, distinct, and specific cost-cutting and revenue-enhancing recommendations. It is difficult to find any recommendations that have been implemented. The David Packard Commissions report on defense management, *A Quest for Excellence,*[4] was received with enthusiasm but never implemented.

Communities will knock on the organization's door to promote their community affairs that eventually will be brought down to the organization's operating level. You may be asked to provide a representative to some community project. While these organizational efforts are necessary, they need to be scrutinized so that the resources provided by the organization provide a benefit in some form. All of these external influences have their rightful place in the organization psyche but they need to be controlled.

THE LOST-TIME REPORT

To demonstrate these sources of lost time, develop a personal lost-time report for the next ten working days. This is not a major program and it doesn't need any computers. It only needs paper and pencil. The purpose is to give you an idea of where you are spending your time. The process is very simple: you're looking for trends, not precision. Just write down everything you do for ten days and the approximate amount of time spent on the activity. You will be surprised by the results. The sole purpose is to find out where you're spending the majority of your time. Is it on the minutiae or on the real work of the manager? This report is only for you. Just check the time spent:

- ❏ On the telephone
- ❏ Searching Web sites
- ❏ Reading and responding to e-mails
- ❏ In meetings
- ❏ On productive work
- ❏ Following up on activities
- ❏ Working with your people
- ❏ Looking at future requirements
- ❏ Away from the office
- ❏ Interacting with professionals and other managers
- ❏ On organizational activities

A review of these items may force you to reappraise where you spend your time and also find a way to offload some activities to others. If you're spending an excessive amount of time interacting with your staff, find out why. Is it because they lack the required competence? Is it because of turf battles? Is it because the department has no clear-cut picture of just where it is going?

LEARNING TO WORK EFFECTIVELY AND EFFICIENTLY

There is no doubt that there is a great deal of pressure placed on achieving results, and it is necessary to focus on results if the organization is going to meet all of its financial obligations. We want our paychecks on time. Suppliers want to be reimbursed on time. The various levels of government also want their share. So it becomes important for managers to scrutinize work methods in relation to effectiveness and efficiency. New tools are available but we need to make sure we're using the right tools and learn how to use them and not abuse them.

Work has taken on new dimensions. Secretaries are generally available only at the executive level. Other high-income professionals hunt and peck and click and drag. Everyone has a terminal with unlimited access. E-mail communication often takes precedence over face-to-face communication, even when the people are within ten feet of each other. Much of the information people view is useless or at least not related to the job. Too much emphasis is placed on precision when precision isn't required. I have always been astounded at what happens during financial reviews. A simple question is asked about the percentage of some figure in the spreadsheet and all the calculators start clicking. Somehow the ability to make mental calculations no longer exists.

Did anyone ever teach you how to work? Probably not. Many years ago I found an after-school job painting storm sashes. I had painted storm sashes at home many times and considered myself qualified. I achieved my first day's quota and went home to do the usual school homework. When I returned the next day, I was greeted with a very cool reception from the owner. He introduced me to a razor blade and suggested that I remove all the excess paint from my previous day's work. He noted that I would not be paid for this work. So for over three hours I painstakingly removed all the excess paint without damaging the putty glazing. When I finished the owner, acting as a teacher and coach, taught me how to paint storm sashes like a professional.

The owner first showed me how to dip the paintbrush to the right depth in the pan containing the paint, remove the excess, and then carefully apply it at the correct angle without getting it on the glass. He did this several times. But this was not the end of the lesson. He then took my hand in his and repeated the whole process several times. He went through this motion several times and then gave me an opportunity to try my hand. He continued working with me until I mastered the art of painting a storm sash without any need for cleanup. This is what you call teaching. After this lesson I never had to scrape paint off the glass. I not only improved my productivity but also actually enjoyed painting. I became a pro at it.

That experience taught me a lesson that I've leveraged throughout my career. There are managers who espouse the approach of setting objectives and then getting out of the way so people can do the job in whatever way they want as long as they meet the objectives. But this approach only works when people have the required competencies, skills, and attitudes to meet the requirements. As a manager you have a responsibility to teach, and if you don't have the required skill to do so, then find someone who does.

While my earlier example about painting sashes demonstrates what occurs in developing manual skills, the same principles apply to developing professional skills. Assume that you're a manager and you have been asked to submit a proposal for some new work. After some thought you decide to give the responsibility to Mike; although he is a relatively new person in the department, he should be able to handle the assignment. You decide that this project would provide some new opportunities for Mike and test his competence in developing a response to the proposal independently. You and Mike have a meeting to go over the relevant details to make sure that both of you are fully aware of the proposal requirements and the timing. You give Mike a briefing of the proposal and an opportunity to ask questions and raise any issues that need clarification. In essence you think you have an understanding and an agreement on the objectives and the timing for completing the task. Your management philosophy follows the practice: *Tell them what you want and then get out of the way.*

In the intervening weeks, you did not have any specific conversations with Mike about the proposal except the casual, "How's it going, Mike?" And of course Mike answered, "*Great.*" However, after Mike presented a draft of the proposal, you found out that each of you had a different meaning for the word *great*. You read the proposal, and you're disappointed with what Mike presented. So you ask Mike to come in and review the proposal. You really don't think much of the effort. It's just more of the same. There's no forward thinking about the proposal's topic. What will you say to Mike? Will you face up to the problem and tell Mike about your concerns? Will you have the courage to take the direct route and level with Mike about your disappointment or will you take the indirect route? Will you be forthright with Mike and tell him that this is not what you expected and why you're disappointed? Will you challenge Mike to justify his methodology and his conclusions during your dialogue? Will this session be a critique or an opportunity to teach Mike what it takes to develop a proposal? The questions asked should not involve destroying Mike's confidence and your trust. Just stay with the facts and be specific about your concerns.

Two questions should arise from your interchange with Mike. First, why didn't you sit down with Mike in the first place and lay out a more detailed plan? Not necessarily timelines, but items to be investigated, people that might be consulted, and a clear delineation of your expectations that might be quite different from what Mike experienced with other managers. Second, why didn't you check with Mike at appropriate times to find out where he was heading?

SUMMARY

❑ The time wasters need to be eliminated. Finding those sources of lost and never recoverable time and eliminating them can provide added hours for constructive work. As noted in previous chapters, time is an unrecoverable resource so it should be treated with care. This does not imply an excessive pursuit of efficiency, but it does imply a pursuit for effectiveness with the appropriate levels of efficiency. While we normally apply the concepts of effectiveness and efficiency to doing things, we need to apply the same principles to our thinking processes.

❑ Whether or nor people are overworked today is a matter of perception. Maybe we're trying to do too many things. If you're enjoying your work even with putting in sixty-hour weeks, you're probably not overworked. If you dislike your job, you probably consider yourself overworked even in a forty-hour week.

❑ Oncken reminds managers to get some of those monkeys off their backs and keep the monkey population in proportion to the available time to feed them.

❑ When we get beyond the monkeys we need to identify those sources of lost time that prevent us from fulfilling our personal as well as organizational goals and objectives. We need to uncover those sources of lost time that surround us and neutralize them.

❏ Developing a lost-time report periodically tells us whether we're spending our time where we should. We gravitate toward the things we like to do but we need to recognize that the things we do must provide added value at our level in the organization.

❏ Continuous learning, whether achieved through formal education or from experience that forces discovery of new knowledge, will continue to determine the success of our departments. Learning how to think and do the work effectively and efficiently will increase the available hours for productive work.

NOTES

1. Julia A. Welch, Rachel K. Ebert, and Gretchen M. Spreitzer, "Running on Empty: Overworked People in Demanding Environments," Chapter 3 in *Pressing Problems in Modern Organizations*, Robert E. Quinn, Regina M. O'Neill, and Lynda St. Clair, editors (New York: AMACOM, 1999), pp. 59–76.

2. William Oncken, Jr., and Donald L. Wass, "Management Time: Who's Got the Monkey?," *Harvard Business Review*, November–December 1974. Reissued November–December 1999.

3. J. Peter Grace, Executive Committee Chairman, *President's Private Sector Survey on Cost Control* (Washington, D.C.: Superintendent of Documents, Document No. S/N 003-000-00616-6, 1984).

4. David Packard, Chairman, Blue Ribbon Commission on Defense Management, *A Quest for Excellence* (Washington, D.C.: Superintendent of Documents, 1986).

Leadership and Communications

The art and practice of managing requires leadership and communication skills, a breadth of knowledge related to the position, proactive attitudes toward meeting goals and objectives, and personal characteristics that meet the requirements of the organization. We'll consider leadership from the perspective of the newly appointed manager and not the organizational executive. Although the same fundamentals apply, the application of those fundamentals takes place at a very different level. We'll consider communications from the perspective of what is being communicated. The entry-level manager is most likely not leading a department that's looking at the next acquisition or merger or developing the organization's cost reduction plan, and is probably not involved in high-level organizational decisions.

TAKING THE LEAD

The literature related to leadership is vast and full of contradictions. There are probably more than 200 different descriptions of this activity we refer to as leadership. The difficulty in arriving at a set of coherent and acceptable principles comes from the inability of researchers to capture in real time the actions and processes used by managers in leading their organizations. The differences in people and circumstances create this dilemma. Most discussions on leadership consider leadership at the top political and executive levels. They relate to Winston Churchill's and Franklin. D. Roosevelt's leadership during World War II. They relate to Jack Welch as CEO of General Electric. They relate to Louis V. Gerstner, Jr., and the rebuilding of IBM. They relate to Dr. Martin Luther King's leadership during the equal rights movement. They relate to the leadership of Mayor Rudolph W. Giuliani during the September 11, 2001, attacks on the World Trade Center.

Leadership at the entry level is quite different. You're not waging World War II. You're not Carly Fiorina working to merge Hewlett Packard and Compaq into a single innovative organization. You'll be managing the activities of probably no more than ten or fifteen people so your role as leader must be viewed from that perspective: a small department with specific objectives that require interaction with many other departments. Look at leadership as *taking the lead*. That implies that your focus is both on today's work and the future work to fulfill your department's purposes and maintain its viability.

FROM RESEARCH ON LEADERSHIP

What does research tell us about leadership activities? A Center for Creative Leadership[1] survey that included responses from 750 executives showed the following results:

❑ The majority of respondents (79 percent) consider developing leaders as one of the five most critical factors for developing competitive advantage.

❑ Executives (90 percent) are very or somewhat involved with leadership development.

❑ People skills were ranked the highest in importance, followed by personal characteristics, strategic management skills at upper levels, and process management skills.

❑ Personal characteristics rise with management level.

❑ Less than half (42 percent) have created or communicated a leadership strategy.

❑ Less than half (49 percent) have an HR program to support development of leadership skills.

These statistics are both encouraging and discouraging. Executives continually call out for more leadership. While 79 percent consider developing leaders as one of the five critical factors for developing competitive advantage, only 42 percent have created and communicated a leadership strategy and only 49 percent have an HR program to support development of leadership skills. Developing leadership skills involves more than sending people to a three-day course on how to make your employees feel good and at the same time meet the organization's objectives. The missing element in most leadership programs involves defining leaders for what and where.

A study conducted at the University of Michigan in the mid-1980s showed that a continuum existed with managers focusing at high performance at one end and people-centered managers at the other end. However, the results showed that managers of high-performance work groups took considerable interest in their employees' future. A performance-oriented leader would not necessarily have low people orientation.

A similar study conducted during the same time period at Ohio State University found that there were two continuums: a high-performance to low-performance continuum and a high people-orientation to low people-orientation continuum. The leader's behavior could fall on different ends of these continuums. In a follow-up study, agreement was reached by both groups of researchers to describe leaders in two dimensions: the performance and people dimensions. Being high-performance oriented did not necessarily mean low people orientation

The research of Warren G. Bennis and Robert J. Thomas[2] regarding general differences in leadership have found some commonalities based on generational considerations. They have classified leaders as Geezers and Geeks. They suggest that Geezers survived the Great Depression and World War II and sought stability, loyalty, and financial security. Geezers read the "great books," and basically lead through the command and control techniques modeled after the heroic generals of World War II. They believe that the mailroom can be the start of a career that can lead to the boardroom. All it takes is hard work, dedication, and loyalty.

Geeks grew up at a time of peace and plenty and seek a more balanced lifestyle. They were fed television programs on demand; doing school homework became a secondary issue; plagiarism from searching the Web grew at a rapid rate. Their parents were well educated, and many had two working parents, so they did not want for material things. The authors also note that Geeks are impatient to reach the boardroom, but with the demise of the dot-coms that attitude will quickly wane. The idea of offering bonuses to come to work has been replaced with finding a job that might offer some iota of security. Organizational loyalty is a questionable value and they seek monetary rewards. (Note: These statements are somewhat true and somewhat false. Populations are not subject to broad generalizations.)

Bennis and Thomas found four competencies that are common to both generations:

1. *Adaptation*—the ability to adapt to circumstances with certain resilience regardless of the nature of those circumstances. Most organizations fail because they lack the ability to adapt to new environments.

2. *Engagement*—the ability to create shared meaning. The ability to motivate people to take risks and move forward. The ability to create cognitive dissonance.

3. *Voice*—understanding emotional intelligence and perspective. Treating people with dignity and respect. Knowing their possibilities and the limitations.

4. *Integrity*—maintaining a strong moral compass. Balancing ambition, competence, and ethical behavior.

The authors argue that both generations acquired their leadership skills through profound experiences that they call *life-defining moments*: Geezers lived through the Depression and World War II, and the Geeks had somewhat other, more diverse, defining moments. Edith Wharton[3] provides a prescription for learning from those defining moments:

> In spite of illness, in spite of the arch-enemy, sorrow, one can remain alive long past the usual date of disintegration if one is unafraid of change, insatiable in intellectual curiosity, interested in big things, and happy in small ways.

LEADERSHIP MODELS

While much of the research on leadership styles is inconclusive, it does follow some patterns. Edward E. Lawler III[4] provides some insight that can help the newly appointed manager recognize the implications of style on leadership. Figure 7-1 illustrates the relationship between a leader's emphasis on performance and people orientation in a two-by-two matrix.

Figure 7-1. Classification of leadership styles.

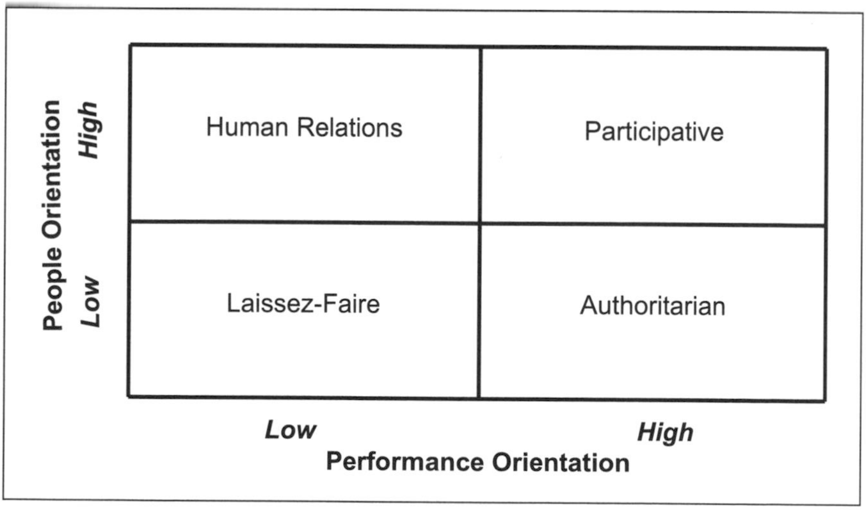

Source: Adapted from Edward E. Lawler, *Motivation in Work Organizations* (San Francisco: Jossey-Bass, 1994), pp. 218–252.

The two-by-two matrix is used for convenience purposes. The four styles include laissez-faire, authoritarian, human relations, and participative.

❑ *Laissez-faire leaders* are basically passive. Personal initiative and risk taking are not on the agenda. As a member of this group, don't expect too much and your group will probably not be recognized as one of the top ten. It may be difficult to make a transfer from such a group. Leaders in this quadrant won't have an impact on the organization. Status quo is good enough.

❑ *Authoritarian leaders* generally make important decisions without input from group members. This is not a viable approach when dealing with professionals—professionals being defined as anyone with specific critical skills. While the authoritarian approach may be required at times, it needs to be used judiciously. Some people respond only when threatened in some way. Most people object to being told what to do and how to do it. However, it may be necessary at times and we need to keep in mind that an authoritarian approach does allow for quick decisions.

❑ *Human relations–type leaders* go to the extreme focusing on people orientation. People orientation cannot be allowed to reach a point where performance requirements are not met and then rationalized. Rationalizing failure to mean success rather than nonperformance merely *dumbs down* the organization. Human relations–oriented managers too often justify all nonperformance, thereby setting the stage for more serious problems.

❑ *Participative leaders* encourage input from group members. Participative leadership, sometimes referred to as democratic leadership, does provide an opportunity to involve members of a group. Bringing in the group to participate in the study and follow-up decision processes does generally motivate the group. However, leaders need to be cautious in carrying the approach too far. Leaders in this category often attempt to reach consensus on every issue; that's an unrealistic approach if meeting the organization's objectives are important. Also, can the group take the time to satisfy everybody's wishes? People need to practice the 80/20 rule; 80 percent of whatever is needed can be accomplished in the first 20 percent of the time.

Keep in mind that the two-by-two matrix shown in Figure 7-1 is for reference only. No manager functions in any one quadrant all the time. Any matrix only provides gross classifications. If we divide each axis by ten we can gain a better appreciation of the matrix. Performance and people orientation do not just exist at *low or high*. There's a range from low to high.

As a new manager you should strive to work in the participative quadrant. As the name implies, it's participation that counts. It's not about reaching consensus on every issue. It is about soliciting input from the staff. It's about working with the people in your department in a collegial style, creating an environment where their work is challenging and where opportunities exist to develop successful careers that benefit the company and the employee. These same opportunities exist in a group doing routine and repetitive work. There is always the challenge for improving some aspect of how the work is performed.

Bruch and Ghoshal Model

Research shows that only 10 percent of managers move a company forward. Such a figure would indicate that the malpractice of management requires attention. The research of Heike Bruch and Sumantra Ghoshal[5] shows that managers squander 90 percent of their time in ineffective activities: only 10 percent of their time is spent in value-adding activities. The study further went on to show that 40 percent were distracted, 30 percent were procrastinators, 20 percent were disengaged, but only 10 percent were purposeful. Their ten-year study with a dozen large companies—including Sony, LGE Electronics, and Lufthansa—showed that too many managers are obsessed with e-mail, meeting mania, and meaningless communication instead of focusing on the real work: new products, new processes, new markets, competition, strategy, effectiveness and efficiency, and the future of the organization.

Bruch and Ghoshal classified managers they studied into four groups: the procrastinators, the disengaged, the distracted, and the purposeful.

❏ *Procrastinators* (30 percent of those studied) suffer from low levels of energy and focus. They dutifully perform assigned tasks but lack initiative or raise the level of performance. Some just cannot get started while others for various reasons feel insecure about achieving the intended results. You probably know which of your professional peers are procrastinators. The study also found that procrastination doesn't totally depend on personality; it is influenced by organizational factors; formal structures with defined job requirements tend to increase the opportunities for procrastination while unstructured jobs tend to reduce the number of procrastinators.

❏ *Disengaged managers* (20 percent) are focused but with low levels of energy. This group is more complex. Some just don't have the inner resources to energize themselves. Some feel that the work assigned is meaningless for them as well as the organization. These managers can also practice a form of denial: they can easily convince themselves that the problem doesn't exist. Others often refuse to take action when needed: protecting their own kingdom takes the top priority. They can be exceedingly tense and are often plagued by anxiety, uncertainty, anger, frustration, and alienation. Organizational processes also affect the disengaged.

❏ *Distracted managers* (40 percent) are well intentioned and highly energetic, but they lack focus. Their mantra might be: *Do something, no matter what, but do something*. This is a group that equates motion with constructive action; don't stop and reflect, just do something. They thrive on *unproductive busyness*. The functional silos breed the distracted manager. They tend to overcommit, become involved in too many projects, and spend most of their time fighting fires. These are the people for whom adding value means keeping people busy. These are the people who create the "make work." The group of distracted managers grows when highly aggressive managers fail to adequately reflect on their actions.

❏ *Purposeful managers* (10 percent) are highly energetic and highly focused: They approach their work from a different perspective. The primary characteristic of purposeful managers is their ability to set the agenda. They extend their freedom to act, manage their bosses' expectations, find ways to accumulate the resources, develop relationships with influential people, and systematically build their competencies to broaden their ability to act. They are not constrained by outside forces or influences such as bosses, other managers, job descriptions, or salaries. They basically define the work and manage the internal and external environment. They set the agenda. These managers put in more effort than their peers, are more aware of the global environment in which they work, select the battles in which they engage, welcome opportunities to pursue new goals, and fully understand the *value of time*. They make time to *think*.

FROM RESEARCH TO REALITY

Figure 7-2 summarizes the issues related to *taking the lead*. Where you position yourself and what philosophy of management you adopt will determine what kind of manager you choose to be. Keep in mind that leadership is but one of three functions of the manager and it is not done in isolation. Managers will not set some specific time to lead. Leading takes place while performing those many administrative duties and while providing direction to the organization. Taking the lead involves being the pathfinder, the visionary, the coalition builder, the doer, the implementer, and means using your power to influence. You look to your staff for ideas but that doesn't absolve you from injecting your own. You as manager set the direction.

A review of Figure 7-2 shows that effective managers are purposeful, as suggested by Bruch and Ghoshal. Can you conceive of yourself being in the procrastinator, disengaged, or distracted categories? Can you conceive of yourself in the laissez-faire, authoritarian, or human relations category suggested by Lawler? Isn't participative management as suggested by Lawler (not democratic leadership), used within a framework seeking

Figure 7-2. From research to reality.

Taking the Lead	Bruch and Ghoshal
• Pathfinder • Visionary • Coalition Builder • Doer • Implementer • Power to Influence	• Procrastinators • Disengaged • Distracted • Purposeful **Lawler III** • Lassez-Faire • Authoritarian • Human Relations • Participative **Bennis and Thomas** • Adaptation • Engagement • Voice • Integrity

input from those who can provide knowledgeable input, the way to manage? I use the term "knowledgeable input" because opinions from those not schooled in the subject are of little if any value. Occasionally someone who knows nothing about a topic may raise a very important issue, but will not have the ability to resolve the problem.

Bennis and Thomas suggest that leadership skills are gained through profound experiences they refer to as *life-defining moments* and we need to be cognizant of these life-defining moments and learn from them. You'll become a purposeful manager when you apply the principles of participative management and practice, you develop the ability to adapt to different circumstances and environments, you create shared meaning and motivate, you treat all people with dignity and respect, and you maintain a strong moral compass. Your career target involves *taking the lead* as a purposeful manager, using the participative approach, and meeting the characteristics of the leader.

FOLLOWERS

Any discussion of leadership involves followers. I believe that in today's knowledge-driven society the word *follower* may be an anachronism. The organizational leader is not giving a command to the followers to *charge the hill* without question. Where such leaders exist, the followers need to look elsewhere for long-term employment. That organization will not be here in the future. Leadership involves building a real sense of collegiality in which participants act as though success depends wholly on their individual input to the project or group. Refer to Chapter 4 for a full discussion of teams.

Those who *take the lead* are the visionaries, the pathfinders, the coalition builders, the ones who make the impossible possible, the doers, and the implementers. They are not just blue-sky thinkers. They balance the need for individual and team performance. They build a sense of trust and collegiality with the group. They build a sense of excitement. The relations are collegial. Their value system includes being the best. The word *follower* doesn't exist.

LEADERSHIP MYTHS

Many myths surround leadership. Leaders are born with certain characteristics. True and false. Everyone can be a leader. Yes and no. Leaders are charismatic. Some are and some are not. Leaders are change agents. Maybe. Leaders are autocratic. Some are always, some occasionally, and some never. Leaders come to the forefront when the situation arises. Probably true most of the time. As usual there is some truth to these myths. Some people are born with leadership characteristics; the young child who displays that innate undefined something that attracts other children. Everyone can be a leader, but not everyone is willing to put forth the effort it takes to be a leader. Not everyone has the characteristics required of a leader. Some leaders are charismatic, although being charismatic is not a condition for demonstrated leadership. Not all leaders are change agents in the strictest sense. Some leaders are autocratic and others are autocratic when necessary. When opportunities do arise for leadership, someone needs to take up the challenge.

COMMUNICATION

Communication skills are absolutely essential but may not be effective if the communicator lacks sufficient knowledge about what to communicate.

So we begin with the premise that the communicator has something to present of importance and understands the subject matter. As an entry-level manager you will not be provided a researcher or speechwriter to clarify communications. You're on your own.

We assume that because something was said, its full meaning has been understood. We assume that if something has been written and then read, it communicated the desired expectations. Every profession cherishes its language and its acronyms. With the advent of the Web we often speak in shorthand without realizing how the receiver may interpret it. When dealing outside our own language we fail to account for differences in meaning. Look back on your career as a professional and recognize how many problems were created from either a lack of communication or a misinterpretation of the communication.

PROVIDING FEEDBACK

Providing feedback involves making a judgment about someone's theories, problem solutions, designs, proposals, or responses to many other requests. Much of today's business literature suggests that judgment be avoided. I suggest that the word management is synonymous with judgment. Managers make judgments based on partial facts, so the ability to make judgments or reach some logical conclusion must become a competency. There are no algorithms that deal with making an assessment and then making a qualified judgment related to some activity. Developing a scale from 1 to 10 and taking an average doesn't work. As human beings we're more complicated.

Feedback without making a judgment provides no value. Keep in mind that we're discussing feedback that takes place every day in every encounter. Feedback can be either positive or negative. It's very easy to provide positive feedback. When all interactions are positive, you as manager will look forward to working with that employee. It's a pleasure to review the work of an employee who has all of the details under control. It's a pleasure to work with the employee who is already contemplating subsequent steps in the process. If an employee meets or exceeds expectations, if a project team exceeds expectations, and if the department exceeds expectations, then the leader can bask in this performance.

But what happens when the individual, the project team, or the department does not meet expectations? Is this a time to provide negative feedback? Most HR people suggest that negative feedback should be avoided and is also counterproductive. I would suggest just the opposite. Negative feedback can be provided diplomatically. If it cannot, then there are other problems that may need to be resolved. Perhaps you need to review some of your past practices in dealing with people. Some managers even develop a habit of congratulating employees even when the work effort fails, and regardless of the reasons for the failure. Perhaps these managers were raised in an environment where failure was considered as a success. Perhaps as children they played on teams where a team that was winning overwhelmingly could not add any more points to its total even if they were entitled to them. Such actions do not build character and such behavior is unacceptable when working with adults.

You cannot put a positive spin on performance that has not met the requirements. You can't fail the person or team based on the results and then give either or both an "A" for effort. We're in the real world. We are no longer in elementary school. You do a great injustice to employees when you do not provide effective feedback. I recall the comments from a supervisor who became very frustrated every time his manager came for a project review. The project was late, there were problems that required resolution, but the manager was praising the team for the fine job they were doing. Such actions on the part of the manager only exacerbate an existing problem.

I suggest that as a manager you use the following guideline: *If you or your team goofed, admit it and learn something from the experience.* Do you want your manager to tell you that your team did a great job when you personally know that your team didn't meet expectations and you didn't meet your personal expectations? You accepted those expectations at the time but for any number of reasons you just didn't perform. So why try to sugar coat a lack of success? Why not admit it and just say we blew it; we'll do better next time.

How negative feedback is presented is important; it cannot become personal, although it is often difficult to refrain from becoming personal if the failure occurred because of a lack of diligence. It's difficult to focus solely on performance when someone fails to perform because of a poor attitude or laziness. However, leaders need to avoid becoming personal in providing feedback. It sends the wrong message not only to the individual but also to the group. What you said to the nonperformer will eventually reach the members of the group and a personal attack only diminishes you as the leader. If you as the manager lose your self-control, you've lost the argument.

A change in performance from acceptable to not acceptable occurs over some period of time. As managers, our responsibility is to recognize any decrease in performance and take the necessary action. The change may have taken place for many different reasons; health and family problems, work assignments, or any number of other issues may be affecting the employee. When these changes are recognized, dealt with, and resolved before they become major obstacles to performance, a great deal of anxiety can be eliminated. A quick response also requires much less effort on your part as the manager. It's much easier to put out a small fire than one that has been allowed to spread.

Feedback is also very important because we sit in meetings and communicate not only verbally but also with our whole physical being. We convey agreement, frustration, disbelief, boredom, and inattention by adjusting our physical appearance in some way: a smile or nod of the head, a lifted eyebrow, twirling or tapping that pen or pencil, and paying more attention to the laptop than the presenter. These actions provide feedback to those engaged in the dialogue. In our one-on-one contacts we convey similar impressions of agreement, disagreement, acceptance, or rejection.

While feedback plays an important role in moving the organization forward, it's basically a study in history. It tells us what happened and allows us to find ways for providing some form of corrective action. The feedback loops required for managing performance are basically the same as those required for controlling chemical and petroleum processes. The many variables in a chemical process are automatically controlled. However, those processes also use what is known as *feedforward.*

What do we mean by feedforward? Feedforward allows us to anticipate the future corrective action based on current performance. As an example, the design of any chemical processing plant uses many control loops with feedback to develop a quality product. Modern process control systems also employ feedforward capabilities to anticipate possible process changes. The emphasis is on anticipation. The feedforward loops anticipate the changes that may have to be introduced because of some predicted error in the system that has escalated over time. That process may be functioning just within specification limits but certain minor changes are occurring that will require modifying other settings if the process is to continue meeting requirements. Basically, feedforward looks to the future.

The following example will clarify the use of feedforward in relation to resolving people issues. You have a review with Tony, one of your staff, regarding some work he is currently doing. Tony's work has really not met the requirements during the past months. As a manager you sit down with Tony and begin discussing his performance. Tony's performance has been well below what you consider an acceptable level. There really isn't anything that Tony has done that's worthy of any kind of praise. If you show your immediate dissatisfaction with Tony's performance, Tony will probably become defensive, you will try to defend your position, and the discussion will probably not yield a resolution of the situation. So the better approach may be to look to the future than to the past. Find some kind of corrective action to bring Tony back on track.

First you need to look at your responses to Tony over the period under consideration and think how you and Tony managed to get into this unfavorable situation. You need to think about some possible solutions before you confront Tony, and you need to get Tony involved in finding the solution. What do you really know about Tony? How much contact have you had with him during the past few months? Is Tony a person who needs close supervision and that supervision was not provided? What knowledge, skills, and attitudes does Tony need to improve in order to meet his objectives? Responses to these questions are solely for your preparation for the discussion. You won't directly confront Tony with them.

If you take the feedforward approach you won't begin by telling Tony about all of the things he lacks to be an effective contributor to the group. Feedforward is about the future. By structuring Tony's workload within his competencies and setting some stretch targets within those competencies you and Tony can begin a new relationship. Tony may or may not accept the challenge. If he accepts the challenge he is probably on the way to becoming a more productive employee. If he resists your alternatives are limited. Termination after sufficient documentation may be necessary. You do need to understand that you have an investment in Tony and should do everything possible to make him a productive employee.

TYPES OF COMMUNICATION

Leadership depends to a great extent on effective communication. The following comments on each of five types of communication will not make you a better communicator but will hopefully sensitize you to the need for improving your communication skills. From there it's up to you. The five types of communication include:

1. Oral
2. Written
3. Graphic and pictorial
4. Listening
5. Reading

Oral Communication

Effective oral communication is not learned from reading: it takes practice, practice, and more practice. It requires understanding the fundamentals of good grammar. It involves developing a vocabulary that allows you to express your opinions, to state your position during a dialogue relative to reaching a decision, to phrase your questions clearly and concisely, and to make your wishes known on any number of matters.

As previously noted, all forms of communication depend on feedback. Feedback between people who are talking includes not only the content but also observation of physical responses. Since the majority of our communication is oral we need to be sensitive to those hidden messages. There is no one in any organization that does not engage in oral communication of some type on a daily basis. For those who report to you intelligent feedback sets the stage for reaching agreement on all issues related to the work effort. Regardless of the topic under discussion there are misinterpretations and misrepresentations that must be rationalized.

Written Communication

We learn to write by writing and not by reading about writing. Written communication takes on many different forms. It includes general correspondence, reports of different types, project proposals, procedures, record keeping, operating instructions, spreadsheet data, announcements, documentation, and presentations. While the technical community is often viewed as having poor writing skills, I have also found accountants and financial people to be lacking in writing skills. We can add to that list just about every profession at every level. Professional staff members frequently labor over even simple project reports. Unfortunately with the elimination of many secretarial positions, professionals no longer have anyone to correct their grammar or rewrite documents. There are no simple answers to resolving this issue. There are plenty of opportunities for learning how to write clearly and concisely but over my years of experience I have not found very many employees taking up the challenge.

The use of e-mail has only exacerbated the problem. I need not dwell on this issue, but e-mail is a major source of miscommunication. In the early days of telegraphy and telex, every word was counted because we paid by the word. Unfortunately the cost per word for e-mail is insignificant, so it's easier to use more words than to develop concise statements. This does not suggest a case against e-mail, but since it is our major mode of communication we need to recognize the need to write with a modicum of correctness. The intent is not to go back to diagramming sentences but to learn just a few fundamentals of good written communication.

Graphic and Pictorial Communication

Graphics and pictures can often communicate ideas and concepts more effectively than the use of a lot of verbiage. However, graphics and pictures must be presented clearly just like any other form of communication. A presentation graphic that cannot be read from the back row of the room provides little if any benefit. Also, too many professionals in all disciplines assume that their audience is as well versed in their topic as they are. So graphics and pictures provide a means for communicating, but they must be explained when used outside the immediate group of professionals.

As a manager you will most likely be involved in making presentations above your managerial level, so make sure that you are communicating to your audience and not to yourself. That diagram or spreadsheet may have meaning to you but does it make sense for the audience? The adage that a picture is worth a thousand words cannot be disputed, but it must be the right picture.

Listening as Communication

Managers need to develop their listening skills. That involves hearing the message and not jumping to conclusions without a full understanding of the message. There are times when we get impatient when listening to the views of others, and perhaps with justification. It takes patience to listen to a boring presenter. It takes patience to listen to someone who is repeating what has already been presented. There are occasions when someone may have to be told to stop talking. The question has been answered and there's no reason to continue the conversation, just cut it off politely. It takes patience to listen to that ill-prepared speaker. But we need to be careful and make sure we're not missing that hidden kernel of truth that may be of significant value.

As managers we may not have control of such situations outside our immediate department's activities. We should make sure that our people do not present similar problems when dealing outside our department. We should try and make it easy for others to hear our message. Good listening also involves good communicators. Can there be anything worse in a time-sensitive meeting than to listen to someone who is focused on what appears to be irrelevant to the discussion or who lacks coherence because of a lack of preparation?

Reading as Communication

In my consulting practice and graduate-level university teaching I always question what professionals and managers are reading. I'm usually very disappointed with the responses. Most haven't read a book related to managing in the last two years, even though they are taking advanced degrees in management. Some do not even keep up in their field of interest. They do not keep up with the daily news events related to their organization's competitors. I hear such responses as, I don't have time, I've heard it all before, and the information doesn't help me do my job.

Reading is an important part of a manager's responsibility. It is a stimulus for creative thought–the kind of thinking required to move the organization forward. We can learn from those news accounts about organizations and their activities. We learn what others have done and are doing. We learn how the actions of others can impact our own operations. Remember the Tylenol incident some years ago, when Johnson & Johnson removed Tylenol from the shelves because some individual tampered with the product, causing several deaths? There are lessons in this decision by Johnson & Johnson that can be transferred to any organization and across all levels of management–ethical behavior, organizational responsibility, and management's response to a major crisis.

So with the amount of information being presented every day, how do managers learn to cope with this mass of data? Managers need to develop some speed-reading skills. They need to be able to sort out the wheat from the chaff. They need to quickly determine what is useful and how to discard the nonessential. The need for speed reading has become doubly important since the introduction of e-mail and electronic communication. Every day we are confronted with information we have not requested. While there is controversy over the benefits of speed reading, it does teach how to scan for relevant information.

SUMMARY

Leadership and communication skills are the two most important skills of the manager. They are closely linked. Leadership cannot be provided without good communication skills. However, leadership as generally taught does not apply to the new manager because the effort focuses on leaders at the upper-most organizational levels. So instead of leadership with all of its upper-level applications, think of your first managerial appointment as *taking the lead*. That will help you keep the role of leadership in the proper perspective. *Taking the lead* means just what the words say; you can't live with the status quo.

The five types of communication are absolutely essential. Oral and written are probably the most important because without them it is impossible to convey a thought, idea, concept, proposal, or solution. Graphics and pictures provide an opportunity to simply sketch out what those thoughts, ideas, and concepts involve. If we don't learn to listen we're doomed not to be able to carry on any kind of successful dialogue in relation to resolving a problem or exploring a new opportunity. Read, read, read! We acquire most information through reading. The faster we can read and comprehend the better. If you're reading poetry, that's a different matter.

NOTES

1. Peter Hapaniemi, "Leading Indicators: The Development of Executive Leadership," Center for Creative Leadership, *Chief Executive Magazine,* October 2002.
2. Warren G. Bennis and Robert J. Thomas, *Geeks and Geezers: How Era, Values, and Defining Moments Shape Leaders* (Boston: Harvard Business School Press, 2002).
3. Comment by Edith Wharton shown on Wharton Center for Leadership and Change Management Website, http://leadership.wharton.upenn .edu/digest/1002.shtml and presented by Kate Faber at kfabr@wharton .upenn.edu.
4. Edward E. Lawler III, *Motivation in Work Organizations* (San Francisco: Jossey-Bass, 1994), pp. 219–232.
5. Heike Bruch and Sumantra Ghoshal, "Beware the Busy Manager," *Harvard Business Review*, February 2002, pp. 5–11.

Thinking Your Way to Success

Action too often precedes thinking. Thinking is hard work and is essential before any group of people can make a coordinated action toward some objective. Thinking doesn't result in something tangible; it's that preliminary work that allows us to consider a problem in its entirety, muddle through the many scenarios or approaches, and then clearly enunciate a temporary path toward fulfilling the objectives.

It's much easier to begin writing a draft than to think through the details of the final manuscript. It's easier to begin doing the research on a new product than to consider the related issues of production and marketing. It's easier for human resource departments to propose development programs than to clearly define the future benefits from that investment of time. It's easier to start doing something than to think about the future consequences of those actions. Since thinking is hard work, we continue to plow the same ground in the same way over and over, hoping to discover something new. So what's wrong with the way we did it yesterday? It worked so why change it? When managers adopt such an attitude they face the consequences of no longer providing value to the organization. When organizations working in a dynamic business environment adopt an attitude that dismisses the need for serious and reflective thinking before doing, its future success may be limited.

The caveat behind thinking your way to success involves recognizing that the test of any organization's work effort is in the marketplace. To meet the challenges posed by the external environment, managers and professionals need to think outside of their own job-specific disciplines. It's not enough to be a professional and disregard the impact of your work on other activities. It's not enough to be a manager and function like a bureaucrat. Both professional and manager need to begin thinking out of the box and be guided by the changes in organizational dynamics. As a newly appointed manager you need to recognize that renewal of *thinking* patterns is the major contributing factor to your organization's success. We usually refer to this as "thinking out of the box." So, how did we get into the box and how do we get out of it? Let's look at the related topics.

- ❑ Becoming an organization
- ❑ Thinking out of the box
- ❑ Moving forward
- ❑ Our changing work environment
- ❑ Getting out of the box
- ❑ Tools and techniques
- ❑ The negative side of thinking out of the box

BECOMING AN ORGANIZATION

Organizations usually begin when some individual takes an idea and through the effort of a small group of people develops a successful enterprise serving some limited group of customers or clients. Through sheer energy and passion, the organization begins its journey on the growth curve. As the organization grows it adds more people and eventually becomes encumbered in policies and practices and beliefs about "the right way to do things." It develops its own best practices and adopts them from other organizations, but at some time in the future those practices can constrain thinking processes. The rules of the game become institutionalized. Those core competencies and capabilities that built the organization soon become counterproductive.

How did the organization get into this box? Figure 8-1 provides a model for discussion of how we get into the box and how we can get out of it. Thinking, motivation, knowledge, and experience feed the box with the expectation of some type of output. Organizations begin with some level of thinking, they are motivated to accomplish some objective, they have most of the knowledge required in the various disciplines, and they gain experience through their activities and provide an output. That output may be positive or negative. Various processes intermingle within that box and over many years become interconnected to the point where they no longer add value. In many cases they constrain the organization's ability to compete. Even though new knowledge and new experiences may have been gained, they have been acquired through the same thinking patterns. There's nothing wrong with institutionalizing ways of thinking or processes as long as they don't inhibit performance. Unfortunately institutionalizing leads to developing a comfort zone where the tough questions related to the future of the organization are not welcome.

Figure 8-1. Getting in and out of the box.

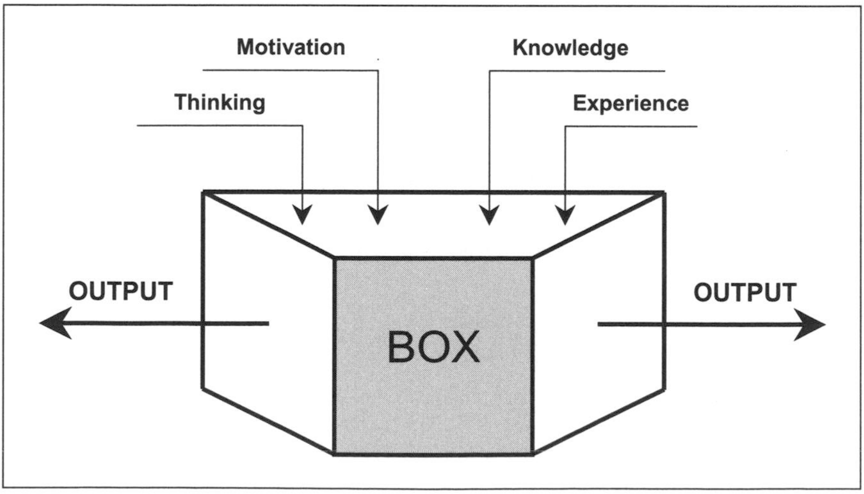

THINKING OUT OF THE BOX

What does this ubiquitous phrase *thinking out of the box* and its variations really mean? In simple terms it means *thinking differently*, or changing our thinking patterns. *Think out of the box* is often used as a metaphor for creative thinking, but to think out of the box involves more than creative thinking. Most thinking out of the box continues to be within the box, occasionally attempting to leave the box but always returning to the comfort of the box. Don't push thinking out of the box too far because it can be dangerous. Changes are coming. However, when former cutting edge ideas become untouchable sacred cows, organizations need to open the box and face reality. Consider the four issues that got you into the box and can get you out of it.

Thinking

Thinking skills involve the way in which people approach a problem and then develop a solution. Too often the problem has not been defined nor has it been framed in such a way that all participants understand the expected results. The integration of the many disciplines required for a successful result is too often disregarded. Assumptions are made without any verification or evaluation of intuition or insight. The basic questions what, why, why not, when, how, where, and who are often disregarded. Thinking doesn't necessarily require a breakthrough in any discipline. It primarily needs the skills to put what is known together in a new architecture or configuration.

We have all heard phrases such as: That's not the way we do it here; You're going against tradition; Why change what's working?; You're looking for trouble if you go down that road; and management (but *who* in management is not defined) certainly isn't going to go for that approach. You can add other comments that you may have been subjected to over your professional career. We do know that these comments constrain thinking and lead to an attitude of play it safe and don't rock the boat. Such an environment leads to certain approved ways of thinking that include:

❑ Thinking too narrowly

❑ Discouraging new thinking

❑ Thinking about everything at the same time without focusing

❑ Discouraging thinking about the next steps

❑ Resisting flexibility

❑ Promoting the company way

❑ Accomplishing tasks through rigid processes

❑ Searching for the best solution rather than the most appropriate solution

❑ Limiting opportunities for creative exploration

You can add to this list from your own experiences. Those rules of thinking are contained in a box that represents a kind of mental prison with various constraint levels that prevent people from fully using their competencies. People become boxed in and play according to the rules.

Patterns for Thinking

Kepner and Tregoe[1] suggest four basic patterns of thinking that people unconsciously use and are reflected in four questions that managers should ask every time a decision needs to be made:

1. *What's going on?* Involves assessing, clarifying, sorting out the details, and imposing order on the problem or opportunity at hand. Separate the complex into manageable components.

2. *Why did this happen?* This thinking pattern relates cause and effect. It prevents us from being at the mercy of our environment. Responses to the question allow us to move forward.

3. *Which course of action should we take?* We need to make choices. For what purpose is the choice being made? Which choice will best fulfill the purpose? Which option is the most productive and requires the least risk?

4. *What lies ahead?* The question responds to acknowledging where the future lies and the future impact of the decisions. Although the future carries less urgency than the present, it cannot be disregarded. Today's actions cannot become tomorrow's problems.

You could argue that this is a simplistic approach to a very serious problem. Not so. These four points are not a prescription. As you ask the simple question, *What's going on?*, consider the breadth of area that it covers. The thinking is up to you and your colleagues. Industry views this question to uncover the financial considerations related to the impact of competition. The academic community might ask, what's going on and what will the university be like in the future? Already, universities are granting degrees where the majority of the work can be done at a location chosen by the student; the living room today, the office tomorrow, next Friday on some sunny beach. What are the implications for the universities? Only a few years ago university deans scoffed at such a suggestion. The various government agencies across all constituencies may also ask, *What's going on?* Why do we have the excessively escalating costs of healthcare and how do we resolve them? *What's going on?* asks everything that needs to be asked.

Question 2, *Why did this happen?*, requires answers but primarily to take advantage of gaining some level of agreement on how we got to where we are. It may be history but useful history to avoid making the same mistakes. Question 3, *What's the course of action?*, focuses on developing solutions with alternatives and selecting the most appropriate within all the constraints. Question 3 must respond to Question 4, *What lies ahead?*

Thinking is not limited to responding to these four simple questions, but all activities are related to one of these four questions. The questions are simple; the answers to the questions are usually complex.

Motivation

Thinking out of the box requires more than knowledge and experience coupled with excellent thinking skills; it requires motivation. Why do you want to dedicate your time and effort and subject yourself to the frustrations associated with disturbing the status quo? If you're really committed to this effort it will consume all your waking hours and more. Thinking about critical issues doesn't stop at 5:00 P.M. and begin the next morning at 8:00 A.M. It doesn't stop on Friday afternoon and then restart on Monday. We know that intrinsic motivation, especially in the person who is always self-motivated, can provide the passion and commitment, assuming the topic is relevant.

Human resource people who continue to argue that money is not an extrinsic motivator should recognize that the money must be there if a long-term commitment is required. Long-term commitments require dedication of personal time. Going around the clock for days and possibly weeks or months can play havoc with family relations. If after all this dedication a person doesn't have the funds to provide some special event for the family, chances are that future activities will be limited to the hours of eight to five. A pat on the back for a job well done is insufficient after hours of dedication of personal time. As a manager you have a responsibility to differentiate between performance levels and that takes judgment. You compensate and provide opportunities to your people based on performance.

Motivation is a more complex subject. How people are motivated and how their interactions contribute to group motivation requires some analysis. Highly motivated people may actually create some level of discord when assigned to a group. Not all members of the group will have the same level of motivation. A group of ten people may have no more than two highly motivated people; the rest will contribute but essentially go along with the majority. The people who wish to take that giant step will be given many reasons why it's better to take incremental steps. The challenge just isn't there. Most organizations function in some type of competitive environment. If nothing else there is competition for funding.

How do you bring everybody on board? There are no seven easy steps for motivating the group. People respond differently. The range of motivators depends only on the creativity of the manager and knowledge about the people involved: perks of different types, praise (which motivates differently, depending on whether it's specific or general), recognition by the group for a job well done, possibilities for advancement, freedom to pursue related activities, access to information, encouragement by management, and fear.

You may question the use of fear as a motivator. Fear from competitors, fear of loss in status, fear of termination for any reason, and fear of not meeting expectations can be motivators. A bit of fear often stimulates the lethargic. However, each of these motivators can also reduce motivation, because not everyone responds in the same manner.

Knowledge

Providing the required knowledge to pursue a particular effort is usually possible and should not create any unsolvable problems. The role of the manager requires the competence to determine the kind and level of knowledge. This is a crucial process that too often is given little if any attention; we think we know our people and the limitations of their knowledge. The general method takes a broad-brush approach and in many situations may be acceptable. But there are other times when it becomes necessary to take the time to determine if the basic knowledge is available. Knowledge involves not only disciplinary knowledge but also knowledge about the organization and the business environment.

As an example, Eastman Kodak dedicated vast amounts of resources to develop the disc camera system. The technology was complex. Other photographic companies also produced the disc camera system under various royalty agreements with Kodak. Kodak introduced the new camera system nationwide on one day with all the resources in place to meet customers' needs. A massive effort. At the same time Japanese companies were introducing inexpensive 35-millimeter cameras that provided customers with better pictures. Needless to say the disc camera never met its expectations. While Kodak had all the technical, marketing, processing, customer relations, and distribution knowledge, it disregarded what was in plain view in the photographic trade magazines: inexpensive 35-millimeter cameras with superior performance that would take over the market. So as we look at the knowledge requirements we must go beyond the disciplinary knowledge and understand the environment in which we're living.

Experience

Experience comes in many different forms from many different work environments. The role of the manager involves determining what kind of experience and at what level. Many different types of experience are available in any group of people, but it's necessary to fully understand the extent and usefulness of that experience. Experience that was gained five years ago is probably not useful unless the person has somehow kept up educationally in the field. If the person needs additional education to get this new experience the project may be severely delayed. It may be more appropriate to find an outside source. Experience must be clearly defined. It must be specific. It is not sufficient to say I need a person with some number of years of experience in a particular discipline. The specific required experience must be defined.

MOVING FORWARD

Like many other management concepts, *thinking out of the box* has become a cliché. Every organization has its thinking out of the box sessions but the results of that thinking seldom meet expectations. You may think that the dot-coms were doing their thinking out of the box but if they were, they left basic principles of managing in the box. They didn't take those principles with them. If the dot-coms had thought out of the box, the dot-com balloons would not have disappeared. Buying new and faster computers doesn't necessarily make us better or more productive professionals. The tools and toys are only performance enhancing when we provide the thinking.

To think out of the box we must wipe our minds clean of what we've done in the past and think about what we'd do today with the advanced knowledge and experience we've gained over the years. Begin the process with a clean and blank sheet of paper and begin turning our thoughts inside out, upside down, left to right, right to left, top to bottom, and so on. We usually acquire that competence by going outside our professional disciplines, observing the real world, and then synthesizing what we observed with all the other knowledge and experience gained from other experiences.

It's like going on a foreign assignment or doing extensive foreign travel. You face new languages, new customs, and new cultures. You quickly learn that you are not necessarily the owner of all the world's greatest thinking and best practices. You learn that people think differently about their personal and organizational lives. They have different priorities and different cultures. Even within the United States we find different thinking patterns as we travel from east to west and north to south. Such experiences help us open up to other ways of thinking. We find similar situations in most countries.

But what does it really mean to think differently? You've started with that proverbial blank sheet of paper; where do you go from here? Can you make a silk purse out of a sow's ear? The process begins by focusing on a particular problem or opportunity and not on some abstract and undefined real problem. I remember too often how many of my professors made such comments as assume friction is zero or assume resistance is infinity. That wasn't the real world that I came from. Defining the concept of *thinking differently* is not really possible but we usually know it has happened when we see the results.

The xerographic copying process invented by Chester Carlson[2] is now over sixty years old. It basically replaced carbon paper. Carlson could have spent his time trying to develop better carbon paper but he chose to think differently. There had to be a better way to make copies. After many years of research and search for funding the invention became the proprietary information of the Xerox Corporation. Xerox became the principal player in copying, lost its position, regained its position, and lost it again. Competitors arrived on the scene and found better ways of implementing the xerographic process. Digital technology arrived on the scene and is now beginning to replace some xerographic processes. Did Chester Carlson think out of the box? You decide.

This example is not about technology; it's about integrating all the different disciplines that make up our organizational structures in order to direct their resources for some defined purpose. The technology, although important, was only the vehicle. Xerography without customers, marketing, finance, and all the supporting entities of the organization would remain a dream. Xerox introduced innovative marketing techniques. They didn't sell the product; they leased the product and collected a fee for every copy. Written communication also changed over the centuries: from hieroglyphics in stone to pen and ink script to the printing press followed by the manual typewriter, to the electric typewriter, to the memory typewriter, to word processors, and finally to computerized word processing with all types of options. Although developing the technology required thinking out of the box, the success could not have been possible without every organizational function thinking out of the box.

Theodore Levitt[3] in *The Marketing Mode* provides an excellent example of thinking differently. Levitt tells us that in the preceding year (probably 1968) one million quarter-inch drills were sold not because people wanted to buy quarter-inch drills but because they wanted quarter-inch holes. The focus went from drills to holes and opened new avenues because there are many different requirements for half-inch holes.

When Jack Welch[4] became CEO of GE he stated his vision for GE in very simple terms: We'll be number one or two in every market or we won't be there. In one of the GE Crotonville workout sessions (that's actually GE University), Welch was told that that vision was preventing GE from achieving some of its growth targets. At one time that market strategy made sense but now that strategy was boxing in GE. The GE Power Systems Group took the challenge. While they had 63 percent of a $2.7 billion market with low growth opportunities, they redefined themselves as an organization that had 10 percent of a $17 billion market but with significant growth opportunities. Welch took the idea and included it in his annual officers meeting and suggested they all prepare a one- or two-page brief to introduce some new thinking.

Most organizations need to examine their thinking protocols and their impact on organizational competitiveness. There are thousands of opportunities to think out of the box. Each only takes one dedicated person to start the ball rolling. As we go about our daily activities we need to think just how thinking out of the box, going through a metamorphosis, or just plain thinking might help us take advantage of new opportunities.

So what does the concept of thinking out of the box imply? How much thinking out of the box do organizations really want? Studies show that most managers proclaim the need for more out of the box thinking for innovation but too often their actions do not support their position. Most managers either directly or indirectly stifle the process or too often kill the messenger. But keep in mind thinking out of the box 24/7 is not required and would only create chaos; it does require risking your reputation, and those risks need to be evaluated. Of course thinking inside the box does provide a comfort zone, at least until someone decides to raise expectations or the next downsizing occurs.

OUR CHANGING WORK ENVIRONMENT

There was a time when most employees worked in some form of bullpen, filled with steel desks and tables, file cabinets, and people. With the exception of managers, scientists and engineers in laboratories, accountants, marketers, and salespeople, and most other employees lived in the bullpen. Communication was face-to-face and within a few steps or a few shouts. It was almost impossible not to become involved with people from other disciplines. The bullpen allowed us to become familiar with what was taking place in the department just by walking around and talking to people in a very casual manner. One walk around the room could provide a great deal of information. Then came the era of the cubicle.

At the beginning the cubicles were used as a means for providing some privacy but as time went on became domains unto themselves with "no trespassing" signs posted. A real comfort zone from eight to five. As time went on, face-to-face communication reached a new low. No need to leave the cubicle, just send an e-mail. All of that interaction in the bullpen was lost. Cubicles tended to become isolation booths and thinking was directed to the activities in the cubicle. No need to find out what's going on in those other cubicles.

Tom Peters[5] recommended the idea of management by walking around (MBWA). MBWA was later also known as management by walking about, and management by wandering around. MBWA is more difficult when everyone is isolated in a cubicle. It's very difficult for a manager to gain an appreciation for the spirit of a working group or to gain a sense of how people work together when everyone remains isolated in a cubicle. Fortunately some organizations are now beginning to develop working spaces based on project needs. This approach allows grouping people with common interests in one location—a small bullpen.

Dilbert has had much to say about cubicles. The prototypical Dilbert complained to his manager one day about the fact that his cubicle had been decreased in size by two inches. The manager responded: "We installed real-time status adjusters in the cubicle walls. Sensors monitor your work and adjust the *cubicle size* according to your value." In the last frame, Dilbert and his coworkers are encased in tiny boxes. "It's amazing how fast you get used to it." Moving from the bullpen to the cubicles has restricted opportunities for people even within a single discipline to increase their breadth of knowledge and understanding.

GETTING OUT OF THE BOX

Not everyone will choose to get out of the box. Managers may attempt to push people out of the box, but that requires creating a new and radically different work environment. In the latter part of the twentieth century fewer and fewer people were willing to give personal time for organizational activities. Subsequent organizational downsizings, the bursting of the dot-com balloon, and a very slow-growth economy only exacerbated the situation.

Figure 8-1 shows the integration of thinking, motivation, knowledge, and experience leading to some form of expected output. Thinking and motivation are the two critical factors. Without them knowledge and experience will stagnate. These four components that put us into the box must somehow be changed to get us out of the box. Integrating these four components requires integration of people, management, and attitudes. Keep in mind that the box involves not only generating new ideas and concepts but also finding ways to implement them. Some level of expertise in problem solving or opportunity finding in the field is also essential. Managers who wish to have their people get out of the box need to develop a culture that allows the out of the box thinkers to function.

If people are an organization's most important asset they need to be treated accordingly. That involves setting high performance standards, identifying the critical mass of talent required to meet the purposes and objectives of the group, building high levels of trust, establishing and maintaining integrity, promoting excellence, promoting teamwork while recognizing individual contributors, and insisting on accountability. This is a culture that will allow those people who have those supposedly *off-the-wall* ideas to take a leadership role in the future of the organization and with guidance from their manager build a forward-looking team.

Managers set the direction for developing an appropriate culture by their actions. Those actions begin with their own thinking out of the box and include defining the purposes, objectives, and strategies of the organization; focusing attention on organizational unit outcomes; communicating appropriately at all levels; providing leadership that focuses on doing; developing operational discipline; introducing change where and when required; taking acceptable risk, making timely decisions, and anticipating the future. A manager who fosters these actions will have little difficulty developing a culture that then focuses on out of the box thinking. The attitude with which people approach their work makes a significant difference. The people and management components are linked by positive attitudes. Unconcerned, dispassionate, or perfunctory attitudes prevent the development of a proactive out of the box thinking culture. There are a few critical attitudes that define a culture: a sense of excitement about the group's activities; flexibility and freedom to those who can manage it; appointments based on competence and performance; motivation from managers by example; performance appraisal based on well-defined objectives; and opportunities for exploiting personal initiatives. Imagine working in a blah environment, with no freedom to act, where performance appraisals are perfunctory, with no defined objectives, and no opportunity to exercise personal initiative. Not a very inspiring culture for a professional in any discipline.

To make the transition to a thinking organization requires going through a metamorphosis: going through a profound change. Individuals through their creativity and persistence change the game. I say creativity and persistence because creativity without implementation provides little if any value. A great dream without the drive and tenacity to pursue it to a conclusion does not add any value. Implementations of new ideas that invalidate current thinking or actions drive this metamorphosis.

TOOLS AND TECHNIQUES

There are three important tools for helping us get out of the box. They include focusing on creativity, using effective brainstorming sessions, and developing workable scenarios.

Creativity

Creative thinking must go well beyond connecting nine dots without making any intersections or determining how many different ways a square can be divided to contain four equal parts. These are interesting exercises and demonstrate some principles but do not help in finding creative solutions for complex problems. So keep creativity training in perspective. Edward de Bono,[6] a well-known researcher on creativity, claims that his concept of lateral thinking can generate almost an idea per minute in three hours. Such idea drops provide little benefit in most situations. Ideas from people who know little or nothing about the complexities of the topic under discussion can provide a great deal of noise, but not much substance. Such sessions seldom resolve an issue and especially when looking back at the consequences of the decision on the total system.

But don't discount de Bono. Edward de Bono differentiates creativity and lateral thinking. Creativity is a value judgment and may be viewed in many different ways. What may be creative to one person may be very ordinary to another. A creative person may be successful in expressing and communicating a special perception of an issue or event that allows others to view the issue or event from a new perspective. But that person may be locked into that special perception. So a person could be equally creative and rigid at the same time. This does not diminish the value of their creativity, but the rigidity could be counterproductive.

Lateral thinking involves the ability to change perception and to keep changing perception. Edward de Bono defines lateral thinking as pattern switching within a patterning system. It's the ability to look at things in different ways and continue the process. Obviously the number of iterations would depend on the scope of the issue or event. We tend to think along one track. We establish certain limitations and worship them as though they could not be changed. They served our purpose well in the past, so why not now? Very often it becomes necessary to move to another track. Give up track "A" with its restrictions and see what's available on track "B." It may be necessary to continue exploring new tracks until a solution can be found that meets the short- and long-term requirements.

Organizational success depends on the creativity that eventually leads to innovation. Innovation is not about ideas. Innovation involves taking an idea, developing it into a workable concept, putting the pieces together in an invention, and implementing the invention.

Innovation = Invention + Implementation/Commercialization

Invention does not necessarily mean acquiring a patent. It involves the unique combination of what is mostly known with research to fill in the missing pieces. But creativity begins with a particular mindset. We need to differentiate invention and imitation. Benchmarking an organization's success stories and attempting to duplicate them is not invention. It's imitation. It's thinking down the same track. Invention involves finding a better way—a way that provides superior benefits; a way that provides those added useful features that the completion lacks.

Brainstorming

Much *thinking out of the box* begins with someone recommending a brainstorming session. But brainstorming sessions usually occur after someone has pushed the panic button. Seldom are they planned with meeting specific goals and objectives. These panic-driven and short-term brainstorming sessions, while providing a quick fix solution for the problem at hand, do little to develop a culture that thrives on thinking out of the box. Brainstorming sessions directed toward the organization's future potential require providing a means for reaching that future. But a single session will most likely not meet the requirements. As a newly appointed manager you play a key role in determining not only your department's future but also the organization's future. A brainstorming session limited to two or three hours where participants only make suggestions will not provide much benefit if the issue is important.

For brainstorming any major issue I recommend the Gaynor approach, which requires isolation for extended periods of time without interruption and without a time limitation and requires the thoughtful development and analysis of alternative scenarios. The objective of a brainstorming session should be the development of a plan that can yield the expected solution. Several sessions may be necessary to reach a final acceptable plan. Answering the four questions suggested by Kepner and Tregoe requires people knowledgeable about the issues and capable of doing the research to find the information that may be lacking. Brainstorming does not begin with a group of people pushing a particular agenda. It involves purposeful inquiry and exploration of new ways to accomplish some objective. You need the right people and preparation for the session.

Exploring New Scenarios

Out of the box thinking involves exploring new scenarios. In our search for solutions we too often jump on the most apparent solution without giving sufficient thought to its consequences. Developing several scenarios allows further consideration of alternatives. Scenario development is a simple process. The objective is to look at several approaches to resolving the same problem but from different perspectives. Not all managers will accept the idea of preparing scenarios. Scenarios confront managers with the realities. Their judgment has served them well in the past so why bother.

Assume that you're attempting to introduce some new activity or a product or process in the group that you manage. You know that any new idea will be met with resistance from someone in some sector of the organization. That's a given. You also know that if the proposal lacks definition someone will find the flaws in your thinking and your approach. So why not explore possible solutions rather than take the most obvious but not necessarily the most effective solution for the long term. While this approach may add more work at the front end of a project, it pays off a large return when seeking approval and during the implementation phase.

Writing scenarios is no more than exploring alternatives, but in a more systematic manner. But those scenarios are not prepared for upper-level management. They're your tools to make sure that you've made the most appropriate choice. They provide you with an opportunity to make the choice after the scenarios have been documented and analyzed. There could be a scenario developed for the quick fix; let's get this thing out of the way and we'll hassle it out at a later date. There may be a short-term fix that explores the roots of the problem. There may be another scenario that considers the short term but makes provisions for future enhancements. And there may be a scenario that looks at the long term. Selecting the short-term fix while providing for the long-term needs may be the appropriate scenario to follow. As I mentioned scenarios are your tools but don't get management involved in them. But if asked what alternatives you've considered you should have no problem answering related questions.

Scenarios also help functional groups such as research develop more realistic proposals. For example, when research and development begins developing a new product, do they consider the impact on manufacturing facilities? Their effort can be directed toward either using existing manufacturing facilities or providing new facilities. The approach to the research would be quite different in both situations. The research time may be reduced considerably if the group is not locked into current manufacturing facilities, while it may take more time if existing facilities are to be used. Well-developed scenarios answer such questions. The process for developing scenarios is not much different from what you may be already doing but is formalized into some form of document to provide guidance. Competent professionals and managers need such a document. The process includes:

1. Developing a statement of the problem
2. Developing appropriate scenarios to solve the identified problem
3. Analyzing the scenarios
4. Identifying the common elements from the various scenarios and evaluating them
5. Going through as many iterations as necessary
6. Selecting the best scenario
7. Stating your reasons and rationale for accepting a particular scenario

The process of scenario building is straightforward and doesn't need any explanation except step 1, developing a statement of the problem. Unfortunately this effort seldom meets the requirements. Scenarios cannot be developed until the problem is really understood.

Here's a real-life example from Lawrence Gibson[7] to illustrate how much effort can be misdirected because of an inadequate statement of the problem. It involves the French subsidiary of General Mills, Biscuiterie Nantaise (BN). There were several competitors for an after-school chocolate cream-filled snack called a *gouter*—a cookie. BN had the most popular brand of the *gouter*. Prince, a fancier more expensive *gouter,* was an aggressive national competitor. But BN's sales slipped for two years and then dropped significantly. BN managers attributed BN's weakness and Prince's strength to a lack of advertising. The solution: Increase the advertising budget. All over France competitors were gaining market share. BN's price relative to competitors was decreasing.

Some questions were raised: What has been done to reduce product cost? Response: We started to recycle broken cookies and changed to less expensive ingredients, and the quality deteriorated. Analysis: BN faced a product problem, not an advertising problem. But something more was needed to regain market dominance. BN took a multiple-flavor strategy, testing various types of chocolate and fillings. Result: Different children preferred different flavors. BN was positioned to take advantage of these different taste requirements. The strategy yielded the expected results: The BN sales decline was reversed, market share rose, and margins improved on the volume gains despite higher product costs. Moral of the story: Don't spin your wheels solving the wrong problem. The original statement of the problem was not defined. The problem was the reduction in quality that had been forced by making cost reductions in order to lower prices and meet sales targets. Not a very good strategy. The research to identify the real problem cannot be a guessing game.

THE NEGATIVE SIDE OF THINKING OUT OF THE BOX

Is there a negative side to thinking out of the box? It depends. Organizations that function on the leading edge and are the leaders in their particular domain have an almost *built-in thinking out of the box* approach but they don't emphasize it. The very fact that they're on the leading edge gives them an opportunity to continue on the leading edge. The word *complacency* does not exist in their dictionary. However, not all parts of any one organization will be on the leading edge. So the concept of thinking and rethinking from new perspectives must become a way of life.

Thomas Kuhn[8] tells us "we shouldn't think 'outside the box' . . . until the box is wholly shattered." Unfortunately such an approach may be too late for a successful recovery. Michael Lewis[9] writes that a new corporate language has been invented to support people's need to believe that their work is actually an endless quest for originality. Before we attribute every novelty to be thinking out of the box we might consider his statement that:

Outside the box is to our age what plastics was to the 1960s. The one thing that is certain is that anyone who uses the phrase *out of the box* is as deeply inside the box as a person can be.

Lewis makes a very good point. By considering everything as being out of the box thinking we trivialize the concept.

SUMMARY

☐ Thinking, motivation, knowledge, and experience are essential to providing an output; these are the issues that get us into the box. If those thinking patterns remain constant for too long they decrease motivation and lessen the ability to gain new knowledge and experience.

☐ Kepner and Tregoe provide us with four basic patterns of thinking required to meet the organization's purposes and objectives. Just ask the questions, what's going on, why did this happen, which course of action should we take, and what lies ahead?

☐ There is no accepted definition for thinking out of the box; perhaps it's indefinable, but we certainly can see its impact when it does occur.

☐ Not everyone is capable of thinking out of the box. If you're passionate about some issue and have the facts and the courage to pursue that issue the criticism and perhaps accusation of disloyalty will not be a problem. They'll jump on your bus when they see signs of progress.

☐ The tools and techniques for thinking out of the box are important, but they cannot be substituted for the integration of thinking, motivation, knowledge, and experience.

☐ Thinking out of the box is a unique competency, so let's not trivialize it by applying it to every ordinary activity.

NOTES

1. Charles H. Kepner and Benjamin B. Tregoe, *The New Rational Manager* (Princeton, N.J.: Princeton Research Press, 1997), p. 9.
2. M. F. Wolff, "Carlson's Dry Printer," *IEEE Spectrum*, December 1989, p. 44.
3. Theodore Levitt, *The Marketing Mode* (New York: McGraw-Hill, 1969), pp. 1–27.
4. Robert Slater, *Jack Welch and the GE Way* (New York: McGraw-Hill, 1998), pp. 59–67.
5. Thomas J. Peters and Robert H. Waterman, *In Search of Excellence* (New York: Harper & Row, 1982), pp. 121–125.
6. Edward de Bono, *de Bono's Thinking Course* (New York: Facts on File, 1982), pp. 53–70.
7. Lawrence D. Gibson, "Defining Marketing Problems," *Marketing Research*, Spring 1998.
8. Thomas S. Kuhn, *The Structure of Scientific Revolutions*, 2nd edition (Chicago: University of Chicago Press, 1970).
9. Michael Lewis, "The Artist in the Grey Flannel Pajamas," *New York Times Magazine*, March 5, 2000.

Measuring Your Chances of Success

Research doesn't give us specific information as to why managers succeed or fail. There are too many different kinds of management positions with very specific requirements and responsibilities that cover a continuum from simple to complex and from routine to very creative and innovative. Managers span the whole spectrum from competent to incompetent. You will also find that the actions of some managers who were considered competent at the time only generated a new set of problems for the future. Yesterday's successes became today's problems.

Organizational history teaches us much about the organizational successes and failures. If viewed with a critical lens, history may help us develop a roadmap for success and also help us avoid some commonplace failures. Your success as a manager depends on the success of your group. That success or failure depends on using a set of appropriate measurements called metrics.

FEAR OF FAILURE

Failure unfortunately is a necessary condition for accomplishing anything. If a person has never made a mistake, chances are that that person has never accomplished anything of significance. Making mistakes and learning from them is part of the success equation and cannot be avoided. But while mistakes are important to success, the types of mistakes need to be considered. Mistakes that occur because of a lack of attention or a slovenly approach to detail are not acceptable. Mistakes that add new knowledge or in some way ratify what is known are important. Thomas Edison once remarked that *every mistake was one less experiment that had to be performed that would lead to understanding.* A child doesn't learn to walk without falling many times before that first step is taken. We make many mistakes before we learn how to participate in any sporting activity. We accept the bruises we get from mistakes made as we learn to ski. But we don't look at these mistakes as tragedies that require some form of closure. Learning to manage is no different, except that now you have a greater responsibility to others than you had as a professional. You are now expected to take risks in pursuing the group's goals and objectives and that involves making mistakes in judgment.

EXPECTATIONS BEFORE MEASUREMENT

As much as we may dislike the need for measuring performance the fact remains that measurements provide a report card about how we use resources. We need some way to keep score about the results achieved using assigned resources in specific activities. We need to know if the use of those resources added value to the organization's purposes and objectives. But before performance can be measured, expectations must be clearly defined. And herein lies the problem.

Too often expectations lack specificity and clarity and thus cannot be measured. Developing those expectations involves what I refer to as doing the *up-front work*: looking at the pieces, their interactions, and their impact on the organization's purposes and objectives. Too often action precedes thinking about the consequences of the action. Look back at your own experiences and think how many times the lack of clearly defined expectations prevented you from accomplishing objectives in a timely manner. Defining expectations also involves thinking about how those expectations will be achieved. Just ask some simple questions that are often difficult to answer: Why are we engaging in this particular activity? What are the benefits if we're successful? What is the organizational impact if we just decide to disregard it? What are the consequences of disregarding the potential knockouts, those pieces of the puzzle that cannot be found?

Meeting individual or group objectives may or may not add value to the organization. The marketing department develops a marketing plan for a new product rollout but the product is not accepted in the marketplace. The government attempts to develop a national healthcare plan (a major project but still a project) and fails. Extensive studies are made, accepted, and put on the shelf without any intent of implementation. Meeting project specifications, schedule, and cost targets may or may not be sufficient.

Is it possible that all individuals met their expectations but the department failed to meet its expectations? Yes. Is it possible for all departments of the organization to meet their expectations but the organization fails to generate the expected results? Yes. What if every department met its performance targets but the organization failed to meet its performance targets? Performance targets, whether related to individuals, departments, or the entire organization, must be integrated into some workable framework. So it's important that managers think beyond following directives and put on the organizational hat and think about the impact their department has on the organization's output.

Avoid those war rooms with the multiplicity of charts measuring every conceivable activity. Gathering data on a multitude of issues that have little if any relevance but might be nice to know has a negative impact on the staff. Besides, war rooms are time wasters. Also the selected metrics should come from available organizational information. You don't need to appoint a metrics specialist. Most groups require no more than five to seven measures to describe performance. We could also argue that there is only one metric: *Did you do what you said you'd do?*

WHAT IS OUTPUT?

What is output? Output is simply a measure of the performance of assigned resources used in specific activities. The challenge is to find reliable metrics for measuring the performance of the assigned resources. Metrics must focus on reality. Too often managers focus on activities rather than the results achieved from pursuing those activities. In academia increases in enrollment, the number of new courses offered, the number and importance of the research grants, and awards for academic excellence tell us little about the contributions of the assigned resources. A more appropriate metric identifies the impact or the potential impact of the learning from those new activities on some segment of society. Likewise the addition of staff or capital investment doesn't satisfy the requirement of a metric. It's the results gained from that investment in staff and capital that provides the metric.

Government agencies may use a metric of increases in funding, expansion into new areas of interest, additions to staff, and number and size of projects completed. As an example, transportation departments often use the number of miles of new highways or service projects completed as one of their metrics. All this tells us is how many cubic yards of concrete have been poured and how many tons of steel have been used for reinforcement. It doesn't tell us the impact the investment had on resolving traffic congestion. A more appropriate metric identifies the results achieved from adding those concrete ribbons. Other appropriate metrics might include improving effectiveness and efficiency of all operations, eliminating projects that no longer add value, and evaluating all processes to eliminate redundancies.

Industry has a very simple metric: net profit after taxes. But that metric will probably not apply to a typical department. The metric may include performance to budget, but is that sufficient? Probably not. It depends on the particular situation and whether the organization looks at short- or long-term performance. Remember the quality mania that took over industry in the mid-1970s? Not that those improvements in quality were not necessary; on the contrary. But some organizations began counting the number of quality circles without paying attention to the output of those quality circles. Not a very good metric. The not-for-profit world cannot use the number of donors contacted as their metric. The number of donors represents activities, not results. More appropriate metrics might include the net increase in funds received, the funds received per personal contact, or the reduction in cost per dollar received.

QUANTITATIVE AND QUALITATIVE METRICS

Most metrics have a quantitative and a qualitative component. The quantitative components include the hard numbers and the "yes" and "no" decisions. The qualitative components are based on judgment and are subject to different responses from different decision makers. The hard numbers provide one measure of performance that while very useful do so with certain limitations.

All organizations in some form or another and with different degrees of discipline operate by using a budgetary process. The process involves measuring income and expense, comparing budgets to actual performance, and any number of other financial criteria. All accounting systems, regardless of sophistication, measure what comes into the organization, what goes out of the organization, and how much is left at the end of some cycle. Comparisons can be made in relation to people count, revenue per person, investment per person, surplus of revenue minus expense, on-time completion of projects, amount of rework both physical and mental, and many other criteria depending on the type of organization.

There is no one set of metrics that adequately describes the department's and the organization's performance. Every organization has its own set of priorities, its own culture, its own focus, and operates within a limited but specific environment. However, there is more commonality of issues among various organizations than we might expect. Performance can be measured by quantified metrics such as "yes" and "no" if we're only concerned whether the objectives were met. We may also measure project performance by using the three project requirements of meeting specifications, delivery, and cost. Common quantitative metrics include:

- ❑ Meeting financial targets
- ❑ Meeting cost reduction targets
- ❑ Benefits from improving products and processes
- ❑ Results from effective and efficient use of resources
- ❑ Improving customer and supplier satisfaction
- ❑ Introducing new products
- ❑ Reducing waste and rework
- ❑ Fulfilling the requirements related to administration, direction, and leadership

- ❑ Making judgments and decisions
- ❑ Providing the resources and developing the infrastructure
- ❑ Developing subordinates

The results from each of these activities can be measured. These metrics may change as the organizational dynamic changes regarding what defines adequate performance.

Quantitative figures tell us what happened in the past. They're figures that we use to predict future performance but they're not realizable at the moment. Every organization hopes their future projections will become real but until they're fulfilled they're only future projections. We have all heard from the financial advisors that past performance is no indicator for the future. The same applies to all organizations. Who anticipated the demise of the dot-coms? Who anticipated the destruction of the World Trade Center? Who anticipated collapse of Enron and WorldCom, the stock market decline, and the downsizing of Silicon Valley? Unanticipated events such as these prevented realizing someone's future predictions of performance. While each of these examples involves negative organizational results, the departments within those organizations played a role because that's where the action took place.

The key is identifying the opportunities and then measuring progress. Look for figures that relate to the subject matter; measurements need not be accurate to the decimal point. We're not planning on sending a man to the moon. Measurements that can be quantified are preferable but we must be aware that what we are counting adds value.

If depending solely on quantitative metrics, keep in mind that today's targets might have been met but future opportunities might have been destroyed. Targets were met but in the process split the organization into various self-serving constituencies. Targets were met but the organization's collegiality was destroyed. Targets were met at the cost of deteriorated relations with suppliers. Targets were met but future government actions may negate the benefits. Laws and directives were abrogated. Targets were met but with questionable ethical practices. Actions such as these can be destructive. So, while meeting targets is absolutely essential in a globally connected world, certain practices cannot be tolerated. Qualitative metrics are judgment calls and provide the added dimension.

QUINN'S LIST

There are also metrics that have both a quantitative and qualitative component. Quantitative metrics are essential but not sufficient. Quinn and colleagues[1] conducted research of managers from 117 organizations, concluding with a list of twenty-one operational problem categories faced by managers. The input came from working managers who are expected to meet certain specified objectives every day. Resolving this list of problem categories in the context of the organization's purposes and expectations is the starting point for developing the needed information for evaluating performance. Not every issue involves every organization but selecting those that do apply and developing a performance scale will provide a metric. I have added four additional problem categories that significantly affect performance.

This list of twenty-one-plus-four problem categories, as shown in Figure 9-1, can be considered from both a qualitative and quantitative perspective, but the quantitative requirements may not be rigidly applied. Each problem category is followed by several questions that allow you to focus the

Figure 9-1. Critical operational issues faced by managers.

From Quinn et al.

Competitive external pressures	Overworked people
Lack of strategic direction	Conflict and intimidation
Multiple accountabilities	Corrosive political climate
Chaotic job rotations	Underemployed human
Unmanaged growth	resources
Poor financial performance	Cultural misunderstanding
Process problems	Unresponsive headquarters
Dissatisfaction with quality	Lack of innovation
Inadequate resources	Overemphasis on analysis
Disappointing sales	Inaccessible information
performance	Resisting globalization
Difficulties in partnering	

Gaynor Additions

The cost of mental rework
Organizational infrastructure
Use of technologies
Systems approach

issue more closely on your department. You may choose to add or refine these problem categories to meet the needs of your department and then develop some scale of measurement, such as 0 to 10; important or not important; did not meet expectations, met expectations, exceeded expectations; or whatever fits the requirements of the department. A response to these categories by the department or a group of managers will raise many questions, but until there is some agreement on the importance and status of each it will be difficult to gain a clear picture of where the department and the organization are heading. I'm using the Quinn et al. list because it's based on research and provides a view from real-life managers. The results are shown in decreasing level of importance, but your priorities could be quite different.

1. ***Competitive External Pressures***. All organizations compete for resources, for talent, for position, for market share, for reputation, for recognition, for its service to the community, and more. Knowing or preferably anticipating the level of competition allows the manager to take the lead and plan for the future.

   Questions: Is competition a factor in your department's area of responsibility? Who are your competitors? Are you leading or playing catch-up? Do you really know and understand their strategy and operations? What are their advantages? What can you do to take the lead? Are you competing within your own organization or accepting the status quo?

2. ***Lack of Strategic Direction***. Every organization needs to know what it wants to be, where it wants to go, and how it plans to achieve its purposes and objectives so it needs a well-defined strategy that points all departments in the right direction.

   Questions: Does your department have the appropriate strategy to accomplish its goals and objectives? Does the strategy provide for taking into account the dynamic changes related to economic conditions, introduction of new technologies, and developing markets? Are those strategies documented and communicated? Note: Beware of strategic planning sessions that yield binders of wishes rather than actions required to take advantage of new opportunities.

3. *Multiple Accountabilities*. The theory or practice of eliminating multiple reporting relationships may be an unreal expectation in a global economy, so we may need to develop the skills to be accountable to different entities. Never in my career have I been accountable to less than two people, and I never encountered any serious difficulties. As a manager you need to be sensitive to the fact that some people cannot function effectively when reporting to more than one person.

   Questions: If multiple accountabilities are an issue, have you identified the people who can and cannot function in this mode? Do you understand why they cannot be accountable to more than one person? What do you do to eliminate any problems because of multiple accountabilities? Are you as a manager comfortable with multiple reporting relationships?

4. *Chaotic Job Rotations*. Removing people from a job assignment at an inopportune time can create chaos either in your department or a related department. There will be times when a rotation may be absolutely essential but managers should recognize the consequences of their decision. Emergencies should not become the operational standard. Avoiding inopportune rotations requires anticipating the future.

   Questions: Is there a backup plan, either inside or outside the department, in the event a key person is recruited for a new assignment? How would you respond if upper management insisted on a transfer of a key person?

5. *Unmanaged Growth*. Managing growth creates a major challenge not only for the organization but also for the department. Yes, there can be unmanaged growth within a department. Managers like to increase headcount, thinking that such actions somehow enhance their position.

   Questions: Do you have a plan for developing the right mix of talent, which might include adding, transferring, or terminating? Do you understand the amount of effort required to bring new people into the group? When adding staff do you consider eliminating the programs that no longer provide a benefit?

6. ***Poor Financial Performance***. When the money spigot is turned off problems increase at record levels, hours of valuable time are wasted talking about the problems, the issues are seldom laid out on the table for total examination, and piecemeal programs are put together to resolve the problem instead of providing the major surgery that may be required. This applies to all departments and organizations.

Questions: As a manager, how will you respond to a decrease in your department's budget/forecast? Do you really need that full budget/forecast to meet your results? Does the budget/forecast specify specific projects? Do you have a backup plan for contingencies that may arise?

7. ***Process Problems***. All organizational processes play a major role in determining the organization's sustainability. Processes guide an organization in meeting its objectives, they provide a level of consistency in performing certain functions, they allow those schedules assigned to the goals to be met with a minimum of confusion, and they prevent reinventing the wheel many times a day.

Questions: How familiar are you with your department's processes (from product genesis, distribution, and administration) and the organization's processes that affect your department? Are your department's processes documented and do they reflect current conditions? How do you resolve complex process problems?

8. ***Dissatisfaction with Quality***. Every organization cannot help but focus attention on quality; the quality of its products and services (every organization has these), the quality with which it treats its customers and clients, the quality with which it recognizes its employees, the quality of its management, and the quality of the many interrelations that allow an organization to meet its goals.

Questions: Does your department have quality programs that include all disciplines and functions? Does your department fully understand the impact of not meeting quality requirements? Is there a method for measuring performance quality? Does your department fully understand the cost implications of not meeting appropriate quality standards?

9. *Inadequate Resources*. Resources will always be limited, but using available resources effectively and efficiently can alleviate much of the shortfall and can provide opportunities for innovation. New knowledge and new technologies such as simulations and modeling can be used to provide the information that might lead to substitutions. The adage that necessity is the mother of invention continues to have relevance. But also keep in mind that resources do not only include people and money: resources also include intellectual property, technology, time, the distribution channels, customers, suppliers, and all external resources.

Questions: Are you and your staff knowledgeable about the available resources provided by the organization as well as those available externally? How much effort is invested at the not-invented-here (NIH) approach? Please note that NIH is not just related to the technical side of the organization; it begins at the top and flows throughout the whole organization.

10. *Disappointing Sales Performance.* Every organization sells something. Industry sells products and services; academia sells educational programs and programs to expand facilities; government sells programs to the citizenry; the not-for-profits sell the benefits of their activities through fund raising programs; professionals sell their ideas to their managers; and managers sell ideas up the organizational ladder. Everybody sells in some way. Selling is not a dirty word.

Questions: How would you rate yourself, your staff, and your organization on selling ideas and concepts to others independently of where they fit on your organizational pyramid? What do you do to teach your staff to do a better job of selling their ideas and the needs and directions of the organization? As a manager do you insist that your staff practice their selling skills in the operations of the department?

11. **Difficulties in Partnering**. Partnerships whether internal or external succeed or fail depending on the people involved. Partnerships by their very nature require a give and take in the decision processes; equal distribution of workload; the ability to resolve conflicts rapidly; less reliability on the letter of the law; and a special relationship between the partners that allows for flexibility and agility. Keep in mind that people working on a project are partners.

Questions: Does your staff develop both internal and external partnerships to the benefit of your department and also the organization? Do your project people work as partners and develop a sense of collegiality? Do you manage the department as a partnership?

12. **Overworked People**. Overwork appears to be a common complaint but the question must be asked whether people are overworked or never learned how to work. Do we mean overworked by the number of hours worked or the perception of being overworked due to other factors?

Questions: Are effectiveness, efficiency, and economic use of resources in all activities stressed in your department? How much benefit are you receiving from the introduction of new information technologies? Do you introduce new technologies and continue to use the same old tired processes? What have you done to decrease the amount of data overload? Do you know the number of hours spent because requirements were not adequately defined?

13. **Conflict and Intimidation**. Conflicts are bound to arise in any situation where different disciplines are brought together to resolve an issue. Lack of a common language among disciplines is only a minor part of the problem. Of course conflicts can involve any number of minor or serious issues. There is only one way to resolve conflict and that involves putting all the issues out in the open to be dis-

cussed without excessive amounts of emotion; I say without excessive emotion because emotion will inevitably be involved to some extent. In situations where two immovable objects are involved, someone must come in and make the decision.

Questions: Do you generally "kill the messenger" who brings bad news? Have you and your people faced conflict openly or paid the price because of lack of candor? How often does serious conflict arise and regarding what types of issues? How would you rate yourself and your staff in regards to managing conflict?

14. *Corrosive Political Climate*. We need to be cautious in using the phrase "corrosive political climate." Wherever there are two or more people politics will play a role but it need not be corrosive. When politics reaches the point where lack of trust, self-serving behavior, and lack of cohesiveness dominate any situation, then the manager has few alternatives. We will find occasions where regardless of the amount of effort dedicated to resolving a situation among a group of people no one makes a move to help. This may be a time for coaching or a time for practicing command and control. If command and control is required the only option may be termination or transfer of the immovable objects.

Questions: Are you sensitive to the political issues in your department and when necessary can you make the difficult decisions? Do you know how to avoid the impact of destructive politics? It can take years to develop trust and cohesiveness in a department and seconds to destroy it. Are you sensitive to the issues and actions that may be leading to developing a corrosive environment?

15. *Underemployed Human Resources*. The underemployed and noncontributors not only generate added costs from their inaction but also from the time they waste for their colleagues. The underemployed soon begin to lose their motivation and eventually become the noncontributors at both real and emotional cost to the department and the organiza-

tion. People need to be given stretch targets in order to keep them employable. This is especially true of people whose work is routine and requires little thought.

Questions: Can you quantify the number of actual underemployed and noncontributor hours in your department and hold them to some acceptable and appropriate level? Do you have a means for identifying the lost hours? If you have underemployed and nonperformers in your department, how did they get that way? Can you provide any guidance that would make them productive employees? Do they remain because you lack the courage to act?

16. ***Cultural Misunderstanding***. Culture, as noted in Chapter 4, plays a role in a department's performance. Working across national cultures requires added sensitivity to the needs of those cultures. That does not mean subjugation to every wish of the cultures. There are no mysteries in working with different cultures. It only requires some effort to know and understand something about the culture. From personal experience I have found that a mix of people from other cultures will eventually develop a culture of its own that somehow blends the cultures into a new one that satisfies the requirements. Unless people and organizations learn to communicate effectively, misunderstandings will occur.

Questions: If involved in cross-national activities, do you have an interest in learning about the culture and at least some rudiments of the language? How would you coach your people if they were involved in cross-national activities? Have you had instances where crossing national boundaries was essential and, if so, what did you learn to do and what not to do in the future? Cultures within an organization can be quite different; can you accept those differences and still maintain good working relations?

17. ***Unresponsive Headquarters***. In recent years most headquarters are beginning to realize that they are not the infinite source of all knowledge and wisdom. Those people across both oceans do have something to contribute beyond being

told what and how to do something. At the same time headquarters, what I like to call the *motherhouse*, will dominate
in the final decision. That's reality.

Questions: What is the attitude of your organization and
your department when dealing with headquarters? If you're
in a position that requires working with the motherhouse, do
you give up on the first try at selling a concept or do you try,
try, and try again and again until you get the required attention from headquarters? Do you have a plan that might include someone at headquarters to assist you?

18. ***Lack of Innovation***. Innovation is one of the most difficult
issues facing organizations. The stakes are usually high,
there are significant risks and uncertainties, and it takes an
exceedingly astute management to listen to the constructive
mavericks and allow them the personal freedom it takes to
innovate. Innovation is not about generating ideas; it's about
doing, or taking an idea and bringing it to fruition. Innovation
is about conceiving an idea, building it into a saleable concept, and implementing it. No implementation, no innovation. As a manager, innovation will be expected from you
and your staff. If it's not expected it might be advisable to
update your resume.

Questions: What would your innovation index be? If there is
no innovation within the department, how will you go about
promoting it? As a manager do you treat everyone equally
or do you make allowances for the most productive contributors? Do you and your staff understand the implication of
being innovative? Do you have those productive mavericks
that will determine the future of your department? As the
manager will you provide the freedom and resources to
sponsor innovation? For a full discussion of innovation, see
Innovation by Design.[2]

19. ***Overemphasis on Analysis***. Analysis is essential but synthesis of that analytical work cannot be avoided. But just how
much analysis do managers need? Follow the 80/20 rule.
Eighty percent of the required information can usually be

acquired in twenty percent of the time. The issue is getting the right eighty percent. Only measure what you need and then use your judgment. No computer will provide the answer. You cannot avoid making judgments on many different issues, that's why you're a manager. If the computer could make the judgment you wouldn't be needed.

Questions: How do you approach analytical studies? Do people who do the analysis have any knowledge about what they're analyzing? Are the analyses in any way being compromised because of certain known preferences by upper management? Do the analyses take into account the system or do they deal with single issues?

20. *Inaccessible Information*. The organization owns the information, so why isn't it available to those who need it? Human nature somehow manages to interject itself and information is held closely and not available for distribution. Withholding information when needed only adds cost. I remember a case in which a division vice president refused to give an upper-level manager the opportunity to review a strategic plan for information that was needed.

Questions: Following the approach of *need to know*, do you and your staff limit distribution of information or any intellectual property? Do you have a policy on free flow of information? What has lack of accessible information cost your department and the organization? Is information available though some formal and standardized database or is it difficult to find when needed?

21. *Resisting Globalization*. Most organizations have little choice but to go global. The mother country is no longer the source of all knowledge and it is no longer the source of all expanding markets. But going global creates a great deal of uncertainty for the organization; it needs to learn how all those other countries do business. The requirements are different. A very successful product in one country may require modification to be sold in another country. Governmental regulations vary from country to country and require compli-

ance. While many difficulties can arise and need to be resolved the alternative to resisting global involvement is stagnation and eventual dissolution.

Questions: Has lack of global involvement by your organization had a negative effect on performance? Is your organization currently involved in any global activities and if not, should there be an effort to become involved at some time in the future? Is there a general interest on the part of the employees in your department to become involved globally? As a manager you know that going global involves an investment of resources, will you invest those resources if justified?

The ranking of these twenty-one issues will vary depending on the type of organization. You may disagree with the rankings for your own organization but this is what the managers reported. It is also difficult to go through this list and find any one issue that does not apply to all organizations and departments at some level. The order of importance may be different but the issues exist in every organization. Now I'd like to add some issues that I have uncovered in my years of experience.

THE GAYNOR LIST

1. *The Cost of Mental Rework.* Rework is not limited to parts, assemblies, or equipment, or to any other manifestation of technology. You may question the issue regarding mental rework. Unfortunately mental rework in this age of the knowledge worker has taken on new dimensions. Months of work may be relegated to the trash bin because of a lack of communication. Project proposals may be reworked many times because of a lack of discipline in defining the requirements. Reports may be rewritten because of a lack of writing skills. Those legal documents may confuse rather than enlighten so are reworked. Lack of timely decisions may involve reworking many documents. All mental work

involves thinking, but thinking requires some form of disciplined process in order to limit the mental rework. There is no measurement that captures the loss due to mental rework. But being cognizant of the mental rework and looking at how many times documents that derive from rethinking are changed do provide some measures on which to take corrective action.

Questions: Do you track the cost of mental rework in your department? Do you have a defined program to reduce the mental rework? Has the mental rework become a source of frustration and lowering of motivation? Have you as a manager been the source of the rework because of undefined expectations and delayed decisions?

2. ***Organizational Infrastructure***. While a department may attempt to interject changes into the organization's operations it may be limited by the lack of a supporting infrastructure. The organization's infrastructure includes purposes, objectives, strategies, organizational structure, guiding principles, policies and practices, management attitudes, management expertise, support for innovation, acceptance of risk, communication, and social responsibility. If the organization's purposes, objectives, and strategies are not clearly defined and communicated, a department may be wasting resources. You need to consider purposes, objectives, and strategies (POS) as a unity. Independently they have little meaning. In pursuing a program that may not be consistent or sanctioned by the organization's POS, a department may be diverting resources that might be used in some other program for a greater organizational benefit. This doesn't mean that the department should not pursue such a particular program, but that the other elements of the infrastructure must support such actions.

Questions: How do you rate your organization's infrastructure? Based on the disciplines and purposes of your department, how do you rate your department's infrastructure? Does it support the department's members?

3. *Use of Technologies*. In recent years our workplaces have been inundated with all types of technological marvels to improve productivity. Some have been successful while others never produced the desired results. Some of this technology could be replaced by pencil and paper. Our ability to store vast amounts of information electronically allows us to develop archives that often contain much useless information and only creates the need for more investment in technology. Think of the hours sometimes wasted by our inability to speak to a person directly, instead of going through endless automatic switchboard choices only to reach the wrong person or be disconnected. Not a very productive way to provide customer service. I'm not suggesting the elimination of technology to improve performance, but I am suggesting that implementing new technologies be based on financial payback just like any other investment.

Questions: Are investments in workplace technologies governed by financial payback? Are those payback estimates real or imaginary? How do you monitor the payback benefits? Are the new technologies just automating old processes or eliminating many of the process steps? Have you turned those cubicles into printing plants instead of selecting what goes electronic and what goes in print?

4. *Systems Approach*. Systems can be defined in many different ways but very simply, a system involves the interaction of two or more people, objects, or entities in pursuit of an objective. The system satisfies certain defined conditions. Why the systems approach? Very few activities can be accomplished by a single discipline or by a single individual. The objectives of one unit affect the performance of other units. So the impact of meeting a particular objective in a unit must take into account its impact on other units.

Questions: Does your unit use the systems approach? Does your unit understand the principles of using the systems approach? If you use the systems approach, have you quantified the benefits? If you do not use the systems approach, have you calculated the added costs to your unit?

OUTPUT EQUATION

The output of a unit involves four measures: the output of each individual in the unit, the influence of the unit on other units, the output of other units influenced by the unit, and the contribution of the unit's manager. Or stated simply:

Unit Output = A + B + C + D

where A = unit member output

B = influence by unit on other units

C = influence of other units on unit

D = contribution by unit manager

Keep in mind that output can only be measured by considering the results achieved. Activities such as defining, planning, scheduling, and controlling are simply activities that hopefully will yield a positive output. They add no value just because they're practiced.

Consider the quantitative measurements for items A to D of the output equation. The quantitative part of A, the unit member output, can easily be measured in the finite terms of meeting objectives or meeting the three project requirements related to specifications, timeliness, and estimated cost. The objectives were either met or not met, without any rationalization or equivocation. If the activities of the individual unit members were integrated the unit should have met its objectives.

Let's look at B and C of the equation, the interrelated influences, at the same time because both can be difficult to measure but important. Once again if the objectives and the three project requirements of each related unit are specified, it should be relatively easy to use the "yes" or "no" approach. The major difficulties arise when requirements of each unit are not clearly defined and communication somehow breaks down in the process. Changes made in one unit and not communicated to another lead the list of problems. Interaction of the unit managers now becomes critical. They must get involved in a timely manner.

Measuring the contribution of a manager involves measuring the contribution to the department and the organization. As noted previously, the manager will be responsible for more than managing the activities of the department since the organization will place demands for time spent on organizational activities. The manager's performance in relation to the department can be easily measured. The department either did or did not meet the expected results. But the manager's specific contribution to the output may not be as clearly defined as to allow "yes" or "no" responses.

Measuring the contribution of a manager to the organization may prove to be more difficult but can be simple if limited to the manager's *specific contributions* without attempting to justify or rationalize them. The manager's effort did or did not contribute to the organization's program. Whether a particular organizational activity was successful may or may not be taken into consideration; the real question is whether the manager made a significant contribution to the organization. Sitting on a committee without making a contribution may be an activity, but unless that activity produces some specific results it adds no value. A manager's performance, as an example, in improving the productivity of the organization's administrative activities can be measured in the same way as that used for measuring the productivity in product genesis or distribution functions, as noted in Chapter 2. The same principles apply: Objectives were met or not met.

DEVELOPING APPROPRIATE METRICS

Developing a set of performance metrics for a department requires identifying the role that the department plays in the organization. The metrics will not be the same for every department unless they are performing essentially the same tasks and their expectations are similar. Metrics need to be consistent within a department, but this does not mean identical. All performance expectations will not be the same. But everyone likes to know by what standard they're being measured. Is there anything more simple and direct than measuring the accomplishment of goals and objectives? Of course that implies that goals and objectives are clearly defined and supported by the organizational infrastructure and that adequate resources are provided.

Any approach to developing performance metrics for any department must take into account the purpose of the department, its position within the organization, and its expectations. The metrics for a group of people doing routine work will be quite different from those involved in creative work; contrast the issues related to processing purchase orders and invoices to research and development in any discipline. The metrics for a sales group will be quite different from those applied to a marketing group. The metrics for a manufacturing group will be different from those applied to a design group. The metrics in academia and government will also be different, but both must focus on measurable results and not on activities.

The higher the department sits in relation to the top of the organization the greater the responsibility in meeting the organization's objectives. As examples, a manager in purchasing will have less impact on performance than the manager responsible for introducing a major new product; a facilities manager in any governmental agency will have less impact on performance than a manager who makes the final decision on a contractual agreement for implementing some new information system; and a manager of a fashionable outlet store will have less impact on performance than the manager of the organization's marketing group. Expectations will rise as the group ascends the organization's pyramid and also as the intellectual requirements of the group increases.

All managers regardless of type of organization face a common problem of managing the people issues; too often they fall at the extreme ends of the continuum that spans the *insensitive to the people issues* at one end to those who *justify every act of nonperformance* at the other end. As a group, engineers tend to disregard the importance of building people relationships. However, we can add accountants, lawyers, and managers from all disciplines to this group. No organization lacks its share of rigid managers who focus solely on discipline expertise and forget that it takes more than discipline competence to meet the department's objectives. Rigid thought processes coupled with lack of concern for the human side of managing prevent compromise and accommodation.

On the other side of this divide we have the *people persons* and others who too often disregard the organizational performance expectations; they can justify any nonperformance. They prefer to avoid dissent of any kind rather than promote nonpersonal intellectual dissent in resolving people problems. Let's face it, some people are a problem and the problem child needs to be dealt with. Both of these groups could become more effective: the insensitive to understand the impact of human behavior on performance and the nonperformance justifiers to recognize that meeting organizational goals and objectives comes before implementing unproven and questionable policies, procedures, and practices.

SUMMARY

❑ Department and organizational metrics are basically a report card that shows how the deployed resources performed.

❑ Making mistakes and learning from them is a precondition for success. We learn more from our mistakes than from our successes.

❑ Defining expectations precedes developing metrics. Those purposes, goals, and objectives must be clearly stated.

❑ Output is simply a measure of performance of assigned resources and applies to all organizations. Output measures results, not activities. Going around in circles yields zero output.

❑ Quantitative metrics are those hard numbers that are difficult to dispute unless someone chooses to inflate or deflate them for their own purposes.

❑ Qualitative metrics add that something extra that defines the organization. They respond to the future rather than the past.

❑ The output equation measures what was achieved without any equivocation. These are hard numbers that come from those "yes" or "no" decisions and from meeting project requirements.

❑ It takes time and effort to develop a set of meaningful metrics. The metrics will most likely vary from one department to another unless both departments are involved in the same discipline.

NOTES

1. Robert E. Quinn, Regina M. O'Neill, and Lynda St. Clair, Editors, *Pressing Problems in Modern Organizations* (New York: AMACOM, 2000), pp. 265–267.
2. Gerard H. Gaynor, *Innovation by Design* (New York: AMACOM, 2002), pp. 243–269.

CHAPTER 10

Managing Your Career

Making a decision to pursue a career in management involves a careful analysis of yourself and an understanding of the future implications of that decision. As this book has made clear, managing involves acquiring new knowledge, developing new skills, recognizing the issues involved in guiding human behavior, looking at issues from a different perspective, working with uncertainties, and taking calculated risks. A major overriding change when moving into management involves depending on others to meet objectives. You are no longer responsible for only your own performance. Your level of success depends on how you balance the people needs with the organizational needs. There is no need to fear entering the management track but a realistic appraisal is essential. So let's consider some of the issues.

THE WORLD IS GETTING BIGGER AND MORE COMPLEX

The world isn't getting smaller as many suggest, but much larger and more complex. While communication networks have brought us closer together and provide instant access for global communication, our horizons have expanded far beyond our geographic boundaries. Every organization is somehow touched by global expansion; not just the industries that have expanded across national borders but also academia, government, and the not-for-profit world. As you make the decision to begin the art and practice of managing you enter a bigger and more complex world. The decisions you make now take on a global perspective. There are many more factors that you must take into account in making decisions.

WHAT DO YOU BRING TO THE TABLE?

Building a successful career in managing depends on what you bring to the table and then what you do once you take a seat at that table. But keep in mind that the others seated at that managing table have their own agendas. There are five major components of management competency. They include:

1. Knowledge
2. Skills
3. Attitudes
4. Personal characteristics
5. Experience

Let's consider each of these individually and their relationships.

Knowledge

Table 10-1 shows some of the knowledge required for managing. Filling the gap between what you bring to the managing table and what you need

Table 10-1. Knowledge component.

	1	2	3	4	5
Management basics					
Decision processes					
Appraising people					
Information systems					
Team development					
Meeting management					
Mentoring					
Innovation					
Documentation					
Strategy					
Legal issues					
Virtual organization					
Ethics					
Financial issues					
Putting it all together					

Note: 1—No competency; 5—Highly competent

depends on your particular assignment. If your interest in managing was secondary to your professional status or you had no interest in managing, you may have a difficult time making the transition unless you work with a manager who will provide the necessary and immediate guidance. You'll need a good coach to get you on board quickly. The transition could become a test of your physical and mental endurance. If you are partially prepared and have a desire to become involved in managing, the transition will be much easier.

I have found that the professionals who are competent observers of the organization's environment make the transition without any significant problems. They are not only competent in their primary discipline but have a broad spectrum of interests. They read about and study management issues long before their first managing assignment. Some take formal management courses. They have a yearning interest in becoming managers.

The gap between the knowledge that you have and what you need for managing must somehow be filled. That gap may be filled through enrolling in internal educational programs, various courses sponsored by training organizations, and programs at colleges; going to the library and cracking the books; interviewing managers whom you respect for getting results; and reading the appropriate management literature. I use the word *appropriate* intentionally since much of the management research and literature relates to upper-level executives and you won't be operating at that level in your first managing assignment. You don't need an M.B.A., at least not at the present time. You will need to dedicate much of your spare time to learning to be a manager. Most of the knowledge requirements can be met through short modules that lay down basic principles. If you've succeeded as a professional you should have acquired some of this knowledge.

First-level managers need grounding in the basics. Climbing that management ladder often includes falling off several times before fully understanding the responsibilities associated with the title of manager. Knowledge is only the first step to excelling in any profession. People become professionals in their discipline through knowledge and practice. It makes no difference whether that discipline involves the arts, sports, academic pursuits, or managing.

Skills

Table 10-2 lists a series of skills that are essential for managing. Leadership, communication, and thinking are at the top of the list. The issues related to leadership and communication were discussed in Chapter 7. Chapter 8 considered the topics related to thinking, and Chapter 5 covered the topics related to project management.

It takes time to develop these skills. You may have had opportunities to demonstrate your leadership skills as you pursued your professional career. But that was most likely directed toward leadership in your discipline. Now you have the responsibility to lead a group, which imposes new requirements. You are now accountable for the performance of other people.

As a manager you will undoubtedly delegate the majority of the department's work to others. But delegation doesn't stop at the point of delegating. That's when the action begins and as the manager you're part of the

Table 10-2. Skills component.

	1	2	3	4	5
Leadership					
Communication					
Thinking					
Project management					
Problem solving					
Problem finding					
Influencing					
Selling					
Integrating					
Making choices					

Note: 1—No competency; 5—Highly competent

action. How you become involved is important. Many people will consider your involvement as micromanaging. There is a fine line between managerial involvement and micromanaging, and at times that line must be crossed. You are accountable for the department's performance and you may need to micromanage if you are to meet the goals or objectives. This word *micromanaging* is used very loosely. A suggestion from you may be viewed as micromanaging. But you can't fear being accused of micromanaging if your department is not meeting its expectations. It's not just your reputation that's important, it's the reputation of people who depend on your department's output to effectively perform their work.

Leadership is closely linked to effectiveness in communication. The issue of micromanaging might be avoided if you set the ground rules regarding performance. If on-time performance is the department's mantra, your staff should be aware that there might come a time when you will become involved in directing some activities. No one wants to be in a group that never meets its objectives in a timely manner. No one wants to work on a losing team. So if you communicate an operational philosophy that establishes the priorities you'll have fewer difficulties in dealing with nonperformance issues.

Thinking cuts across leadership and communication. Neither can take place without serious thought—thought that looks at alternatives rather than jumps to conclusions that may create future problems. There are times when out-of-the-box thinking is absolutely essential and there are times when it may not be appropriate. An acceptable level of competence must be developed for the remaining skills listed in Table 10-2. You can't possibly manage effectively without project management skills, problem-solving and problem-finding skills, and influencing and selling skills. You must also integrate activities in pursuit of results and know how to make choices. In your particular position you may need other skills that you will need to identify.

Attitude

Table 10-3 lists the attitudes considered desirable for managing. Adequate knowledge and skills without appropriate attitudes yield less-than-expected results. As noted throughout this book, managing is a people business. Leading a group is not possible without some very specific personal attributes. A focused attitude will yield a focused group. A proactive managerial attitude will yield a proactive group. These are attitudes that not only apply to you as manager but attitudes that should be engendered in your staff. If only you possess these attitudes you'll have a difficult time managing the group. How do you transmit these attitudes? By example, by expectation, by coaching, and if necessary by prodding. The list of attitudes is provided for guidance only. As with knowledge and skills the specific needs for your group must be identified.

Table 10-3. Attitude component.

	1	2	3	4	5
Focused					
Flexible					
Reliable					
Agile					
Proactive					
Sensitive					
Committed					
Self-confident					

Note: 1—No competency; 5—Highly competent

You may be asking yourself, however, what do I do if this list is not in synch with my manager? You may report to a manager who lacks focus, who is rigid, who seldom meets the organization's objectives, who is reactive or inactive, who lacks sensitivity, who doesn't demonstrate commitment, and cannot integrate the activities of the related departments. If such conditions persist, the time will come for making a decision.

You have two alternatives: (1) If you think there's a chance that the organization will go through a metamorphosis and that you have a chance of changing the direction, then stay; and (2) if you think that the organization will not change and you're not willing to work in such an environment, then update your resume. Neither of these two alternatives is very exciting. In alternative (1) you may face several years before any changes are made. In alternative (2) you begin a job search while continuing to work. The point to remember is that it's *your career.*

Personal Characteristics

Let's face it, working with a group of compatible people allows you to move beyond personalities when the panic button is pushed. No one begins the blame game. Everyone focuses on resolving the issue. But everyone isn't perfect. Table 10-4 lists some personal characteristics that can make or break an organization. As a manager you need to be sensitive to these characteristics since they will impact the performance of your department. You can't build an effective group if you compromise on these critical characteristics.

Integrity involves adhering to ethical and moral principles in dealing with others. It also means being true to your own philosophy of managing. Dedication to your work as a manager and fulfilling your commitments sends the message. Honesty cannot be compromised. The truth and nothing but the truth. No game playing with words. Your display of energy and drive will influence others if there's full understanding of where that energy and drive are directed. The thoughtful manager always has the advantage over the one who shoots from the hip. Your display of self-motivation will cause others to emulate your effort if you have the right people. Being respectful to others regardless of level is not a choice; your future depends on it. There is no excuse for being late. If you can't plan your time, then

Table 10-4. Personal characteristics component.

	1	2	3	4	5
Integrity					
Dedication					
Honesty					
Energy					
Drive					
Thoughtfulness					
Self-motivated					
Respectful					
Punctual					
Human behavior					
Curiosity					
Tenacity					
Persistence					

Note: 1—No competency; 5—Highly competent

don't expect others to do so. Your demeanor and conduct and your response in times of conflict or crisis sets the direction of the organization. The cause is lost if the response becomes personal. Curiosity in related matters allows you to look to the future. Tenacity and persistence guide you toward completion of your objectives and desire for additional challenges.

Experience

The experiences that you bring to the position of manager go far beyond what you gained in your professional life. You bring the results of every experience in your lifetime whether good or bad, successful or unsuccessful. Those experiences shown in Table 10-5 influenced your attitudes, affected the development of your skills, and provided an opportunity for gaining new knowledge. Those experiences listed have had an effect on your response to accepting the job of managing. You have most likely encountered managers who span the continuum from competent to incom-

Table 10-5. Experience component.

	1	2	3	4	5
In primary discipline					
In related disciplines					
In business activities					
From observation					
From various jobs					
From avocations					
From living					

Note: 1—No competency; 5—Highly competent

petent, teachers who spanned that same spectrum, and colleagues of various types in the professions. You bring the results of these experiences to the workplace. If you sold lemonade on the corner or delivered newspapers or sold Girl Scout cookies you began learning about people. These experiences had an impact on how you view the world around you. These experiences now affect your personal behavior.

This continuum from knowledge to skills to attitudes to personal characteristics to experiences is a closed loop. Thus, the results of any experience feed back to knowledge (what we learned from the experience) and should improve our skills, reinforce our attitudes, and confirm our personal characteristics.

EVALUATING YOURSELF

Tables 10-1 through 10-5 give you an opportunity to evaluate the five components related to management competency. Complete the information in the tables and consider your ability in these five areas. This is not a psychological test but an opportunity to give you some idea of what you need to do to fill the gap between what's required and what you bring to the managing table. After filling in the data, take a simple average of each of the five components in each category that is of importance to your managing position and plot the results on the spider diagram template in Figure 10-1. For comparison, the completed spider diagram in Figure 10-2 shows

Figure 10-1. The five components of management competency: template.

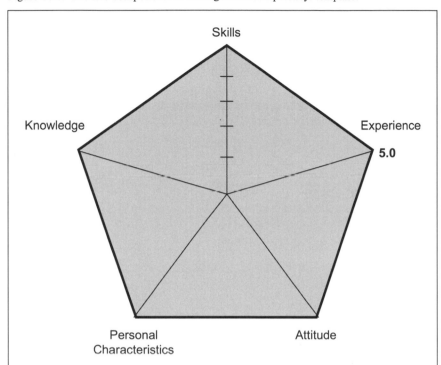

graphically where one manager stands on each of the components and their relation to each other. You will probably not rate a (5) on any of the five components but you should be able to appraise yourself honestly.

The spider diagram gives you an opportunity to consider the five components and decide whether you can make tradeoffs. If you're low on experience but high on the other four components you have a good probability of success. If you're high in knowledge, skills, and experience but low in attitude and personal characteristics you have some work to do if you're going to be successful. If you have good communication, leadership, and thinking skills, demonstrate a moderately good attitude with good personal characteristics, but you're low in knowledge and experience, you can still be a successful candidate for managing. Your skills, attitudes, and personal characteristics would indicate you have the ability to learn.

You may argue that the averaging process can be misleading. True.

Figure 10-2. The five components of management competency: sample.

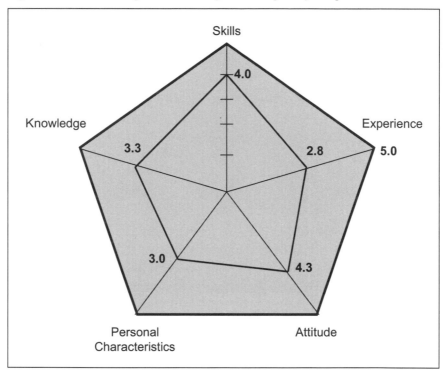

This is neither a scientifically developed nor a psychological test of your ability to manage. This exercise allows you to determine if you should attempt to climb the management ladder. Its purpose is to give you some idea of the expectations from managing and your ability to fulfill them.

A word of caution: as you rate yourself, you should also describe what allows you to rate yourself at a particular level. Think of what you'd say if someone asked you some basic questions about managing and what you bring to the table. Have you made decisions and how did you make them? If you consider yourself an innovator, identify the actions you've taken during your lifetime that qualifies you as an innovator. If you consider yourself as a leader, can you identify when and where you demonstrated leadership skills? Do you really have communication skills? When was the last time you identified a problem and proposed a solution? Ask yourself the same sort of questions to address your attitudes, personal characteristics, and experience.

REWARDS AND PITFALLS OF THE MANAGEMENT LADDER

The rewards associated with the managing ladder depend on why you made the choice to follow that path. If you perceive a job in management as a status symbol, an opportunity for greater security, the additional perks and benefits (there are some), and a play-it-safe attitude by pleasing the next levels of management, then life can be comfortable. Many managers have played this game very successfully. They have managed to milk the cow dry and their managers were blind to what was going on until the organization began missing its performance targets. This condition exists until a new upper-level manager arrives on the scene and begins looking at past performance through a set of realistic eyes. If managing is perceived as a responsibility for contributing to the performance of the enterprise, then managing becomes an intensive process.

Becoming a manager does have its rewards for the person who has a passion for managing. Managing even at the entry level provides opportunities if the manager brings to the position the appropriate mix of the five components of managing competence. Managing is a people business that potentially requires dealing with ambiguities. If you fit the criteria for managing, the satisfaction comes from *making a difference* by accepting the intellectual challenge of leading a group of people in pursuit of some desirable objective.

Larry Bossidy[1] suggests that managers have different kinds of intellectual challenges. Conceiving the broad picture is generally intuitive and, I might add, comes from mulling around many ideas, sometimes for long periods of time. One doesn't define the broad picture by looking out the window and exclaiming, "Eureka!" According to Bossidy, shaping the broad picture into a set of analytical executable actions is a "huge intellectual, emotional, and creative challenge." This is your challenge as an entry-level manager.

The pitfalls of climbing the management ladder depend principally on the organization's work environment. Here are some of the issues to consider:

❑ No more forty-hour weeks—you dedicate whatever time is required.

❑ You are now accountable for performance of your staff.

❑ Demands will be made on your time for pursuing organizational efforts that will add responsibilities beyond those of your group.

❑ The *business* of the organization takes precedence over discipline considerations.

❑ You are the final decision maker for your department unless your manager interferes.

❑ You wear the seven management hats for your department, a new hat for the organization, and are expected to make a personal contribution to the work effort—you not only delegate but also come forth with the innovative approaches for moving your department forward.

❑ People conflicts will arise within your department, the organization, customers and suppliers, and governmental agencies—solve them now rather than evade them.

This is not only the real world of managing but also the real world of the professional who excels in his or her discipline and focuses effort on achieving results. If you've lived with these pitfalls and managed them as a professional then you should have few problems living with them as a manager. They were pitfalls that came with the job as a professional and they also come with the job of managing. These pitfalls go with the new territory but at the same time you can't become obsessed with them and allow them to dominate your life for long periods of time. Learn how to control them.

FROM PROFESSIONAL TO MANAGER TO PROFESSIONAL

The enticement of perks associated with managing often turns out to be something less than expected. What at one time was looked upon as an opportunity to explore the possibilities of latent management talents and the opportunity to make a greater contribution to the organization can become a nightmare. The person who at one time came to work energized by professional challenges now can't develop the energy to carry on throughout the day. Many well-qualified professionals make an attempt at the managing ladder only to find that they're really not suited for the assignment. They just can't seem to acquire a perspective from the other side of the desk. Too often a well-qualified professional begins to become a liability.

Every organization knows the high cost of management malpractice. Moving a professional to the management level without a full analysis of the managerial job requirements and consideration of the five components of managing competence can be a serious mistake. It is a more serious mistake if the professional is allowed to wallow in a management position without a program to improve performance. It is not only the manager who suffers, but also the staff. Both are quickly demotivated even under the best of conditions.

Some managers consider that a return to professional status after failing in managing has no negative consequences, but the reality is usually quite different. Professionals that move to management and then return to professional status return as failed managers. This is reality, and the impact on the individual depends to a great extent on the work environment. Returning to professional status also requires time to become knowledgeable about changes that have taken place in the individual's discipline. A two- or three-year transition period could have very negative consequences considering the changes that may have occurred during the interim period.

FOREIGN ASSIGNMENTS

Do you take an assignment to a foreign country? Most of the comments from returning foreign service employees (FSE) are negative. They focus mainly on what occurs when the FSE returns to home base rather than what was accomplished during the overseas assignment. Having spent seven years in an overseas assignment, having knowledge of many FSEs from other organizations, and also having been actively involved in finding replacement managers and professionals, I found that most complaints were not really justified. Foreign assignments involve hard work and dedication. You and your family are not on vacation. You're working and living in a new culture, there's a new language that needs to be accommodated, and certain local traditions need to be observed. For example, in your new assignment your holidays may be replaced by those of the country in which you're stationed. If you choose to live with your own people—for example, in your *"nation of origin"* village—you'll limit your opportunities for engaging the culture and learning how to relate to and communicate in your new environment. In spite of all these changes there are significant opportunities for professional and managerial growth.

A successful transition to a managerial position to and from a foreign assignment depends on many factors.

❑ What is the purpose of the assignment? Is the objective to continue on the current path or to chart a new path? Each requires different competencies.

❑ What do you bring to the assignment that is not available in the country to which you were assigned? You need to bring something that is needed.

❑ Is the assignment putting you out to pasture because of some internal intrigue or is it one with great expectation? If you were put out to pasture, what is your track record in this foreign assignment?

❑ What is the competence level of the staff and management at the new location? Too often FSEs do not appreciate the available local talent because of different work habits.

❑ Most FSEs go on an assignment without any competence in the language of their new country. Although it's not essential to become proficient, you should at least make an attempt.

❑ Participate in the cultural rituals and you'll find your new colleagues helping you at every turn. Ignore these rituals and you'll have a difficult time building relationships.

❑ Family issues become paramount. One caveat: the spouse must agree if the assignment is to be successful. Those language and cultural barriers must be transcended in some way. Certain inconveniences will be ever present. Life can be very difficult if English is not spoken in the country and the spouse has not had even a minimum of language training and fears attempting to communicate.

Reentry into the parent organization after a foreign assignment depends not only on what was or was not accomplished but also who knows about what was or was not accomplished. Too often FSEs fail to communicate with the appropriate people at the parent organization. You can't afford to lose those contacts and that network of people who thought you were the ideal candidate for that foreign assignment. Maintaining that network is easy today with all the available means for electronic communication. However, in the final analysis your reentry will be governed by what you accomplished, assuming that your organization recognizes some fundamental principles associated with managing their human resources. You also need to recognize that reentry involves some prior planning. An FSE on a three-year assignment should probably begin thinking about making that reentry at least twelve months in advance. You'll also need the full support of your current manager.

So, do you take that foreign assignment if offered? Only you can make that decision. But keep in mind that if you plan to climb the managing ladder to the executive levels that the globalization of most organizations almost demands that you have foreign experience.

THE M.B.A.

Is an M.B.A. a one-way ticket to management? Probably not in most cases. Is an M.B.A. necessary to pursue the management track? Not necessarily. Over the last few decades many organizations have continued to emphasize the M.B.A. degree for managers. There has been a proliferation of M.B.A. degrees to reflect the needs of various specialized disciplines like manufacturing, technology management, marketing, economics, public administration, and many other disciplines. Although these programs are directed at managers or those who plan on becoming involved in managing, they fail to teach the what, why, how, who, when, and where so essential to the manager. We can argue the value of these programs, but all they provide is some basic education about the discipline of management that is not necessarily relevant to the entry-level manager.

Learning about managing is no different than learning about any other profession. An artist masters the art by painting. Knowing how to mix various colors to achieve a particular impact can be learned, but becoming an artist requires practice. A golfer may study and learn about the stance and how to address the ball, but becomes a professional golfer only through dedication and practice. A manager learns to manage through practicing the art of managing.

As an entry-level manager you need some management basics and you'll learn as your career progresses. You don't need a semester's course in financial management for nonfinancial managers if all you need to do is develop a return on investment (ROI) or learn how to put together a budget. You're not the accountant or controller and you shouldn't try to be one, but you need to learn enough about what an ROI is and what should be included so you can communicate with your accountant or controller. Table 10-6 provides a list of some modules that apply to (1) general management knowledge, (2) communications in its many forms, and (3) leadership at the entry managing levels that will help the newly appointed manager get on track more quickly.

WHY MANAGERS SUCCEED OR FAIL

There are obviously many reasons why managers succeed or fail. When talking to managers or to students in graduate programs, I usually ask two questions: (1) How would you describe your current manager? and (2) Do you emulate or would you like to emulate your current manager or any other manager that you know? I'm not suggesting that they be clones of their managers, I'm simply attempting to determine what kind of managers they work with. Seldom do I receive positive responses. Effectiveness and efficiency in meeting the organization's objectives do not appear to be a high priority with their managers. Too few managers have the courage to raise the difficult questions—those issues where executive preferences dominate but are inconsistent with the organization's objectives. So organizations have some serious problems to resolve if they're seeking proactive managers who bring out the best in their people.

Table 10-6. Basic learning modules for entry-level managers.

General Management	Communication	Leadership
Fundamentals of management	Introduction to communication skills	Types of leadership
Working in teams	Communicating the message	Attitudes and traits of leaders
Working as individuals	Understanding the message	Accepting the risks of leadership
Whistle-blower or malcontent	Learning to listen	Demands on the leader
Becoming multidisciplinary	Communicating with peers	The pros and cons of taking the lead
Product development processes	Communicating across disciplines	Demands on the followers
Sources for ideas and concepts	Communicating with upper management	Organizational leadership
Project classification and selection	Communicating with customers	Developing leaders
Documentation	Communicating with suppliers	Organizational infrastructure
Becoming an internal entrepreneur	Communicating across the board	Team leadership
Fundamentals of estimating	Communicating via e-mail and the Web	Doing it differently
Financial implications of decisions	Communicating in meetings	Creating a leadership environment
Working with the legal department	Presenting plans requests for approval	Consensus or what
Effective information systems	Fundamentals for making presentations	Consent or command
The virtual organization	Making the business presentation	Sitting on the sidelines
Taking career risks	Selling ideas and concepts	Motivating others
Systematic development of needed skills	Impact of communication on teamwork	Impact of leadership on careers
Ethics	Developing communication networks	Taking the lead

Your success not only depends on your own efforts but on the support you receive from your manager and executive management. Regardless of how proactive you may be you need an environment that will support your efforts. Success or failure can be personal, organizational, or beyond organizational control.

Personal

Throughout this book I have discussed being proactive, taking charge of your career, living the philosophy of making a difference, putting on the business hat, thinking out of the box and being the constructive maverick when necessary, and doing what you said that you would do. You may consider this an impossible task, but I suggest otherwise. It's possible and is accomplished every day by people who understand the five components of managing and recognize that learning is a continuous process and never stops.

When you meet the requirements of the five components of managing competence (knowledge, skills, attitudes, personal characteristics, and experience) and your staff meets its professional requirements, success of the department is almost guaranteed. Success requires that there be a balance of these five components. If you do not meet the requirements of the five components of managing competence your chances of failure increase significantly. Highly motivated departments are bound to be successful because the energy and drive to succeed is always present. They're the group that sees the glass as half full. You need to recognize that you set the course and through your personal actions send the message that determines whether every issue is a tragedy or an opportunity. Of course you can suffer setbacks when serious problems arise within your department, but managing under such circumstances is the test of your competence.

If the time comes when you become disappointed with your own performance and cannot influence what goes on in the organization, your success and the organization's success will be limited. Your success depends on the efforts of many other people both above and below your level.

Organizational

Managers succeed or fail depending on how the organization manages its affairs. Organizations fulfill their purposes and objectives through developing workable strategies and implementing operational plans. Under these circumstances success is managed. Problems and opportunities are anticipated and solutions are developed in a timely manner. But problems can arise when executive management makes demands but does not provide the resources and infrastructure to meet the demands.

Organizational failure also stems from appointing managers to upper-level positions who never should have been appointed. They may have had the educational credentials but the track record of accomplishments is rather thin. Academic records after five years of experience have little if any significance. Managerial appointments cannot be made from reading the last five performance appraisals. New appointees need to be a known quantity to those making the appointment and the track record is what's important. Organizations fail when the incompetent manage the organization's business. As a manager your opportunities are limited if upper management doesn't perform.

Beyond Organizational Control

Recent events in the global economy demonstrate how careers in managing and in the professions can be either put on hold or destroyed. After years of economic growth, introduction of innovative products and practices, and the birth and death of the dot-coms, the United States faced the September 11, 2001, terrorist attacks on the World Trade Center in New York City, the Pentagon in Washington, D.C., and on American Airlines Flight 93. Normalizing the impact of such incidents goes beyond organizational control. At the same time these incidents need to be kept in perspective. Many organizations were facing financial difficulties that were certainly exacerbated after September 11. Under these circumstances managers require not only added dedication but also the courage to make those difficult decisions. Your success or failure under such circumstances depends on what you bring to the managing table.

SUMMARY

Making a decision to pursue a career in managing requires an evaluation of one's interests, knowledge, skills, attitudes, personal characteristics, and experiences. You do not manage people, you manage their activities. So what issues do you consider as you manage your career in managing?

❑ Identify what you bring to the managing table and what you need to do once you've taken a seat at that managing table. But keep in mind there are others sitting at that managing table who have their own purposes and objectives.

❑ The quality of the five components of managing competence—knowledge, skills, attitudes, personal characteristics, and experience—that you bring to the managing table will determine your success as an entry-level manager and your future in managing.

❑ Climbing that managing ladder requires not only the energy to continue the climb but a passion for dealing with the unknown. Do all managing issues involve the unknown? No. But you need to be able to think ahead of your competition.

❑ The rewards and pitfalls of managing are well known. The rewards are easily accepted. The pitfalls need to be put into perspective. You chose the managing ladder.

❑ You and you alone are responsible for your career. Yes, organizations can help defray part of the cost, but the responsibility is yours.

❑ Moving from professional to managing and back to being a professional can delay advancement in either career. Before making the decision to pursue the managing ladder, ask a simple question: Do I really have what it takes to be a good manager? Only you can answer that question.

❑ Do you accept the opportunity to take a foreign assignment? You know the conditions and the benefits, but only you can make that decision. However, keep in mind the value of foreign experience.

❑ Do you need an M.B.A.? No. What you need is knowledge of the fundamentals of managing. How you acquire that knowledge is irrelevant.

❑ Your success in managing essentially depends on you. There are issues beyond your control, but if you have competencies required to be a manager you'll overcome any problems.

NOTE

1. Larry Bossidy and Ram Charan, *Execution: The Discipline of Getting Things Done* (New York: Crown Business, 2002), p. 32.

Index